FUCK ME: A MEMOIR

for you

Praise for "Fuck Me: A Memoir"

With *Fuck Me,* L Scully has given readers not just the best—and most appropriate —title in recent memory, they've given us an utterly original, unforgettable new voice in memoir: simultaneously wry, honest, utterly direct, and deeply vulnerable. This is a queer coming of-age story told through the lens of sex addiction and two quests, one for lasting love, the other for mental and emotional health. The resulting narrative is laced through with bracing critical rigor and an inventive poetic sensibility. And when Scully's emotions roam beyond words, they include handwritten notes, photos, drawings, and texts from a deep personal archive to suggest what can't be said. The result is a many-layered testimonial to an extraordinary identity-in-progress.

-Pamela Petro, author of *The Long Field: A Memoir, Wales, and the Presence of Absence*

In FUCK ME: A MEMOIR, L Scully unearths the complexities of unrequited love stories and mental health in this tumultuous life of bliss and strife. We ride not only a voyage through gender from high-femme-to-butch-to-femme-as-drag, but also brace the splitting hearts and skin of all parties involved—clinicians, lovers, friends, family, metamours.

Through juxtaposed sketches of relationships graced with the utmost passion and the obscure ways that they end, and relishing femininities with a masculine demeanor, there is an undeniably fazed honesty of sexcapade, yearn, and death in L Scully's FUCK ME: A MEMOIR. The love stories croquet therapized worksheets and dream-like diary entries in such a diligent manner, it makes readers release our memories, too. Strapping feverish revelations of multi-selves of passion and manipulation with humor, lesbian whimpers, and unearthed poetic darlings, FUCK ME: A MEMOIR reads like a gilly of mirrors.

A chronology of how intimately and casually sex and terror are interwoven. How cyclically our desires preempt our dysfunction. How our defensiveness breeds addiction. Fuck Me cuts an uncomfortable autopsy of intimacy - eat or be eaten. L Scully's feat is turning over these stones of everyday catastrophe to reveal the ecosystem thriving beneath, without wincing. There's an inviting blase-ness to the language, a road worn indifference from someone who's been the mouth and the meal. Structurally, I enjoyed the alternating forms of memoir, scrapbook drawings, screenshots, poetry, lyricism. Honest without aggrandizing, Fuck Me will fuck you up, like a forehead kiss after a hard slap.

"Rendered in a fresh, witty, unforgettable prose, Fuck Me: A Memoir explores what happens when people, love and pleasure become akin to addiction. It's a raw account of the yearning that comes with attempting to mitigate the singular loneliness of the human experience. Tender and funny, poetic and vulnerable, L Scully has written themselves into the literary archive of the queer, trans experience."

Fuck Me is truly teeming and masterly. L Scully's writing is so intimate as to make me feel like I myself am speaking it into existence, wearing their rain-damp clothes. Although Scully's memoir posits their own toxicity and strictures, I found myself believing Scully to be totally guileless. That is to say, I fell in love with them. *Fuck Me* is a devouring matrix of romance and addiction. It is a memoir well-versed in what love gives, making us feel both removed from time and more situated in its torment.

- Maggie Von Sacher, author of *Rabbits*

It's late and night; the lights flicker on inside. You find yourself pausing to admire the flawless architecture of the house, which is made of glass. It is made of essays, archived diary entries, stick-and-poke tattoos from an ex-lover--spilling out of its closets are the beautiful, discarded garments of your host's previous gender(s). You realize, of course, that you're inside the house--you, who thought you were outside, watching. Someone takes you by the hand. You can't wait to see where they'll lead you next. Hilarious, unflinching and relentlessly self-aware, Scully does the confessional genre with rare panache, guiding the reader through a history of sexual and romantic entanglements that are sometimes delicious, sometimes harrowing, and always narrated with a stunning and revelatory eye for detail. Intimate and engaging inside and out, *Fuck Me* left me satisfied. And wanting more.

- Mack Gregg

Contents

I will now call to mind my past foulness, and the carnal corruptions of my soul: not because I love them, but that I may love Thee...

And what was it that I delighted in, but to love, and be beloved?

Augustine of Hippo, *The Confessions*

I'm addicted to you.

Britney Spears, *Toxic*

Prologue

It's the first Sunday of August, and I'm in a queer "healing masculinity" morning meeting. I'm sitting in my Boston bedroom on this sunny day in 2021, unmuting my microphone on Zoom. I am twenty-six. *Hi, I'm L,* I say, *and I'm a sex and love addict. I'm humbled to be here.* Fuck, did I just say HUMBLED? Maybe I shouldn't have broken up with my ex-vangelical ex-partner after all; I'm starting to sound like a goddamn Christian. It's a record scratch kinda moment: how did I get here?

The internet celebrity starts us off with announcements, and Ethan, the older trans poet in the group, drops wisdom on how to be in your body. I'm thinking of asking him to be my mentor but I can't tell yet if it's because I am undeniably attracted to him. There are usually between a dozen and twenty people in these Zoom rooms, but it's Ethan whom I want to cheer me on and congratulate me for having the self-awareness and inner strength to come to this meeting in the first place. To tell me FUCK IT, let's ditch this meeting to be together; we can be each other's recovery. Shit, is this what the Zoom room people mean when they say *fantasy addict?* Given my track record, it doesn't feel too far off.

I'm thinking of the time I fucked the host of that sex party, two years back, who was about thirty years older than me. Leo. He had the classic transmasculine charm of looking decades younger than he actually was, and he was visiting DC from LA to host a series of sex-positive educational events, including the party. It was my first time—not my first time having group sex, or sex in front of others, but it was my first time at an explicit sex party. Needless to say, I was nervous. I was attending with my best friend Rita and a new friend, Mayah, who would soon turn out to be the third point of our trinity. I can't remember what I wore, only that I spent hours deciding on an outfit. That happened a lot when I was femme. I suppose it still happens now, but I've lost a bit of the relish that came with doing makeup and my hair. The past year or so I've been

1

presenting more butch, cutting off my long red curls and switching my heeled black boots for sneakers. I only wear dresses now as drag.

I do remember I was in some all-red get-up, which ended up matching the low lighting at the suburban house where the sex party was taking place. We drove into an affluent neighborhood outside of DC, up to a big chateau-style house whose blinds were drawn. We could still see the red light peeking through. *You guys, we're totally gonna get fucking murdered tonight.* My friends laughed in nervous agreement, yet we left the safety of Rita's red Corolla for the unsureness of the red-lit house. I clocked Leo right away. Slender, big brown eyes, wavy graying hair. Just my type. He was co-hosting the party with his partner, whose name I forget, another well-known sex educator and facilitator of such events. When I got there, they seemed like a united front.

We sat cross-legged in a circle, my friends and I toward the back of the room, while Leo and his partner presented the terms of agreement for the sex party: consent, confidentiality, safety. As a warmup we were asked to state to the group of about thirty our "mildest" and our "wildest" for the night. Most people's mildest ranged from holding hands or cuddling on the couch to tying someone up, and their wildest was a cacophony of sex acts: being fucked from behind in a fur suit, group lap-sitting while being tickled, being suspended from the ceiling and whipped. I probably said I didn't have a wildest, knowing me.

After the opening circle, the spectating began. My eyes found the Cat-girl. She wore a flowy babydoll dress, ears and a tail, and I think I recall a painted-on nose. She walked on all fours, only stopping to groom or preen, licking her paws before continuing on to her Daddy. The sounds of her purrs radiated from his lap, and my friends and I looked on in awe. Such a vulnerable display of animal femininity felt at once disturbing as hell and curious, almost attractive. At some point we got caught up in a rope-tying circle, and I pulled Rita's ropes tighter and tighter as Mayah performed sex acts on her. It was lighthearted and fulfilling, fun in its connectedness. The older femme rope top, the conductor of the action, was excellent with her instructions, and the rope bunnies, her willing subservients, were good sports about letting us have a turn. But Leo stayed in the corner of my eye.

Leo's partner seemed to be suffering from a headache and was telling Leo in a corner that they needed to lie down and rescind their hosting duties. Leo, a little concerned, agreed with some good-natured hesitation, and then all of a sudden, the partner was gone, and we were fucking. We were fucking on the couch in the front room for everyone to see. He was wearing latex gloves and put his hand inside me while Cat-girl purred in ecstasy in the background. I assumed Rita and Mayah were where I left them, all tied up. A couple of guys asked if they could watch, and I started to nod my acquiescence and then remembered what Leo said at the beginning of the party: straightforward, verbal communication, no maybes. So, I said I didn't mind, and we had a little crowd going on right as Leo's partner walked back out, looking pissed. I wasn't sure if I'd violated some unspoken rule by fucking the host, or the host's partner, or what, so after we finished, I congregated with some stoners in the bathroom to get high off a fancy vape.

Sex parties, as a general rule, are substance-free, or, at least, good ones are. We said fuck it and got stoned while the hosts worked their shit out in whispers and came back out to eat snacks, hoping our eyes weren't red like the lights. I don't remember leaving but I do remember Leo and I thanking each other for the exchange and a buzz in my head of *holy shit I just fucked that old-as-fuck sex party host and liked it.*

All this to say, I usually get what and who I want. I know how that sounds and I'm not sure if it's my sense of sexual confidence, flirtatious personality, or sheer dumb luck, but when I want something to happen with a certain person, the stars do tend to align. Maybe I'm being too innocent. Maybe it's that I'm an excellent communicator and I know the right things to do and say to get what I want. This is without any malicious intent, and yet still feels inherently manipulative. I guess that's what manipulative people tell themselves in a grand sense of self-delusion. Which is why I'm in this meeting. Calling myself an addict. Healing my masculinity, whatever that means. Taking charge of my addictive behaviors for the first time. Offering myself up as flawed.

A Note

The images, comics, zine excerpts, drawings, and hand-written poems you see in this work are primarily from my college sketchbook (pictured below), which mostly functioned as my diary, from the ages of approximately 18 to 22. Some of the drawings or quotes are by people who were in my life at the time, many of whom I am no longer in touch with. I have kept this sketchbook with me for close to a decade, moving it from house to house, state to state, at some points even country to country. Please note that with these archival images, I am looking back.

Characteristics of Sex and Love Addiction © 1990 The Augustine Fellowship, S.L.A.A., Fellowship-Wide Services, Inc.

1. Having few healthy boundaries, we become sexually involved with and/or emotionally attached to people without knowing them.

2. Fearing abandonment and loneliness, we stay in and return to painful, destructive relationships, concealing our dependency needs from ourselves and others, growing more isolated and alienated from friends and loved ones, ourselves, and God.

3. Fearing emotional and/or sexual deprivation, we compulsively pursue and involve ourselves in one relationship after another, sometimes having more than one sexual or emotional liaison at a time.

4. We confuse love with neediness, physical and sexual attraction, pity and/or the need to rescue or be rescued.

5. We feel empty and incomplete when we are alone. Even though we fear intimacy and commitment, we continually search for relationships and sexual contacts.

6. We sexualize stress, guilt, loneliness, anger, shame, fear and envy. We use sex or emotional dependence as substitutes for nurturing care, and support.

7. We use sex and emotional involvement to manipulate and control others.

8. We become immobilized or seriously distracted by romantic or sexual obsessions or fantasies.

9. We avoid responsibility for ourselves by attaching ourselves to people who are emotionally unavailable.

10. We stay enslaved to emotional dependency, romantic intrigue, or compulsive sexual activities.

11. To avoid feeling vulnerable, we may retreat from all intimate involvement, mistaking sexual and emotional anorexia for recovery.

12. We assign magical qualities to others. We idealize and pursue them, then blame them for not fulfilling our fantasies and expectations.

I. "I Don't Want to See or Be Seen by Straight People"

I'm not going to lie to you: at that very first virtual meeting, I decided I was better than everyone there. Perusing the long list of queer Sex and Love Addicts Anonymous meetings, I opted for the Thursday morning meditation and topic meeting group. At the beginning of the meeting, they asked me to read the twelve characteristics aloud. I nearly choked on the first one. *I don't have poor boundaries,* I thought, patting myself on the back. I was close to typing into the Zoom chat, "Sorry guys, great to be here but I think I'm in the wrong place," and never fucking going back again. Sorry to the person who recommended the group to me via Instagram DM. I don't have an issue saying NO or standing by it. I don't have an issue communicating my needs and expectations of others. In fact, I absolutely have the opposite problem. I stick way too stridently to my expectations of the people in my life, and I'm constantly being told, by myself and others, to lower them. I blame it on being a Capricorn, but you know, I think it's deeper than that.

I remember when I was in my intensive outpatient therapy program in January and February of 2020, almost two years ago now. At the time I was living abroad in Spain and after a very obvious mental breakdown, flew home to Cleveland to stay with my parents while I sought help at a local hospital. I attended the outpatient program for about a month and a half, before "graduating" and returning to Madrid. I arrived at the hospital in my long fur coat from a vintage market in Valencia. I probably looked absolutely ridiculous. But that was nothing compared to my attitude. I was so angry: at the therapists, at my hometown, at the burgeoning pandemic, at the teaching job I had just quit, at the world in general for landing me there. But especially at the therapists. They represented to me a whole lot of trauma that I hadn't been able to touch yet: they reminded me of my involuntary psychiatric hospitalization the previous year, back in DC. And I sure as hell was going to let them know that.

After a couple weeks, though, I got really down with the idea of "radical acceptance." It was mostly a joke at first, but eventually, I started listening to what the therapists had to say, and what they had to say was plentiful. Each week in outpatient had a theme, and each day a derivative of that theme. One such theme was boundaries. I think we spent a whole week on *boundaries.* Of course, I smiled smugly when we got to this part in the program. *I have this in the bag. I can check out.* News to me, however, was that boundaries existed on a spectrum. Shit.

....

I'm sitting in my chair with my feet up, as far to the back as one can be in a semicircle, looking at all these poor people with totally shit boundaries whose loved ones keep walking all over them to varying degrees. Suddenly, I'm flipping the page in my binder to the illustration of the boundary spectrum, and there, across the line from "boundaries too flexible," is something I'd never heard before: "boundaries too *inflexible.*"

God damn it, I think, *I can't cruise through this one the way I initially thought.* If I have one flaw, and let me tell you, I have many, it's that my boundaries are so fucking inflexible. I just never thought of that as a problem and I said as much to the therapist. She looked at me pointedly and asked if I wanted to keep cutting people out of my life once they'd crossed a boundary; some of which were verbalized; some lived in my head. The immediate answer was *yes, fuck them.* And then the gentler answer, the lonely answer, bubbling inside me was *no.* I had a hard time exhibiting forgiveness. I still do. It just doesn't come naturally. But in that moment, in that question, I saw a different outcome for the first time, and it was different from the exponential loss I'd been experiencing in my relationships for the past couple of years. Maybe I could forgive. Maybe my boundaries really were too inflexible. Honestly, that was one of the biggest takeaways of outpatient for me, and armed with that knowledge, I decided I was absolutely going to crush this *boundary* shit when it came to addiction recovery. After all, I had a head start.

Guess what, though? I was so stuck on the *having few healthy boundaries* clause that I ignored the other words making up the first characteristic of sex and love addiction: *we become sexually involved with and/or emotionally attached to people without knowing them.* A name comes to mind; a year comes to mind: Zora, 2018. I met them in the weeks following my breakup with the person I thought I'd marry, Nico. When my relationship fell apart with Nico, I was deeply unwell: suicidal, crying in the bathroom at work, unable to process losing my first queer love - and with that, the first real queer future I ever saw for myself. I was still living in DC, where I went to college, working for little pay at an art gallery, and I desperately needed distraction, so I got on dating apps for the first time. "I just need a good rebound," I said to friends, meaning I needed to lose myself in sex so I didn't lose myself completely.

I actually met Zora because I slept with their best friend. Her name was Violet, and she brought a law textbook to the bar, on our one and only date. We had fumbly sex that left me excited but unsatisfied, and she asked me to please not sleep with her friend, Zora. I agreed. I'm not sure how exactly Zora and I got connected. I'm pretty sure we matched on a dating app, but they asked if I'd like to get drinks as friends. I accepted. Of course, I talked about my intense attraction to Violet, and for some reason, we ended up back at their place. Their tucked-in button-down and perfectly coiffed side-shave were a little more *dapper* than I usually went for, but something about their doe eyes and musical voice caught my attention. They had an embroidery piece on the wall that read, "I don't want to see or be seen by straight people." I knew then that we would fuck. Not that night, but another night soon.

And we did. The details of how it came about are hazy, but we basically decided on *fuck Violet.* Zora arrived at my Capitol Hill house, waited on the porch for me to answer. When I opened the door, we kissed immediately. It was a good kiss, and soon, we were upstairs, entangled in my futon bed in that tiny room, their face lit up by my rainbow fairy lights.

Zora and I quickly became inseparable. Completely devastated by my breakup with Nico, I flung myself headfirst into this new situationship. I thought we had a modern DC romance: I lived in Capitol Hill, they lived across town in Petworth. They had a cerulean blue Honda Civic and would park it outside my house or outside my work, waiting to bring me back to their place. My first indication of the whole poor boundaries thing – and I mean theirs, not mine – was when Zora would come visit me at work. Once, they even skipped their own work to hang around mine.

We were the ultimate DC queer couple: I worked as an assistant curator at a contemporary folk art gallery, and they worked for a major human rights nonprofit. They made a hell of a lot more money than me. And they would idle around my work, taking me to breakfast on H Street after a sleepover, dropping me off and coming in to say hello to my boss. Both the director of the gallery and my manager hated Zora. They thought there was something off about the way they hung around, a little *clingy*. My supervisors made fun of their gender-neutral pronouns and said they looked like a little boy.

At the time, I was a power femme. Meaning I had long curly hair and wore heeled boots with chic dresses and lipstick to work. I wore lingerie to clubs. I relished in my femininity, my hard-won softness, my glittery outsides matched only by my hyper-confident, almost masculine demeanor. In short: I was a fuckboy. *Fuckboy* is a word that technically means a man with many sexual partners, but in the queer community, usually means a masculine-of-center person who will sleep with you and then never text you back. Zora was a known fuckboy. I felt that I had met my match.

10

Zora took me to hotels with rooftop pools for cocktails, nightclub masquerade parties, and lobster dinners. On my end, I looked the part: corseted black dresses and attention-catching earrings, lacy underwear peeking out from my cleavage and the thigh slits in my dress. Sometimes I felt like a sugar baby whose daddy was my same age: Zora wined and dined me, I came back to their bed every night. They paid for my Ubers and made me omelets in the morning, and I dressed up just to crawl into bed beside them. I was enchanted. I was high. I suddenly had everything I could want: the fancy DC brunch lifestyle, someone to drive me to wherever I wanted to go, constant attention, and the best sex I'd ever had. We sent each other roses at work. We also fucked in the bathroom.

At the time, I was a beautiful young woman, and Zora was a dashing nonbinary person. I would walk with them to work in the morning, both of us wearing one of their button-downs, take a picture at security as a company guest and have my face printed on a sticker to grant me access to the nonprofit building. Being an organization that advocates for trans rights, the building was equipped with several gender-neutral bathrooms. In a fit of lust, though, Zora sat me on the sink in the basement women's bathroom and made me feel dirty in the best way. Sometimes I worried if fucking on the job was a sign of poor boundaries.

Like most intense rebound flings, things turned sour quickly. Zora was possessive and insisted on monogamy from me. As someone who has been nonmonogamous my entire adult life, this was no small ask. It evolved into an ultimatum: I accept the terms of monogamy, or we break up. Seemed a little suspicious that Zora suddenly had clear boundaries as it pertained to me being with anyone else. On the heels of losing Nico, I couldn't fathom another breakup. I also couldn't imagine committing to someone so soon after my last relationship fell apart. Meanwhile, Zora was seeing other people too: A tall and beautiful sex worker and a girl in New

York with borderline personality disorder. Zora gave me a lot of reassurance at their expense: I was much better at sex than the sex worker; I was much less mentally ill than the girl in New York.

We hit a rough patch when I went to visit my best friend in Seattle. I made it clear that I would likely hook up with someone while I was there. In return, Zora went to New York to visit the girl who insisted on Zora being her *favorite person,* a term for fixation for those with borderline. Before I left, Zora bought me a vibrator that they could control with their phone. The idea was that I could wear the vibrator inside me on the West Coast, and they would be able to control it remotely from the East Coast. Something about this felt off to me, but something else felt kinky. I leaned into the kinky side of things. I hooked up with a married, trans cowboy in Seattle. We didn't end up using the vibrator.

I can't remember the first time things went to shit with Zora, but I do remember crying in their car while declaring that I loved them and that we couldn't be together. We held each other and sobbed. Soon after, though, we were back at it, unable to keep away from each other during the nights. Zora wrote me a song; the chorus was my name and a lot of "Oh"s. I snuck away from my engagements with friends to end up back at their apartment. The worst thing about Zora was the circle talking. When we fought, which was often, they did this thing where they would manipulate the conversation until I didn't know what I was saying anymore or whether my perceptions were real. One night, we jokingly asked a friend to "peer mediate" an argument about the monogamy thing that got heated. It always ended in sex, that night in my friend's bed.

Eventually, I got tired of hearing the negative things Zora's friends had to say about me, all in the words of Zora themselves. Zora wanted me to see their therapist, which I felt was another aspect of control. We had a blowup that summer of 2018 about all of this, and the last text I remember sending - as a reply to a desperate "I love you," - was "Fuck that, Zora." We never talked again. Despite my fear of being alone after Nico, ending things with Zora, however explosively, was a huge relief. I blocked them, and we stayed in our separate orbits around town. I couldn't afford the lifestyle I was living with them, anyway.

The whole thing lasted about three months. They read me their college diary, and I still can't say that I knew them deeply. I thought I could know them from the inside out. Most of the affair was sex and promises of getting married in Cambridge atop their favorite restaurant's rooftop. My favorite thing about my relationship with Zora is that it ended. And that I don't have to pretend to be into the nonprofit industrial complex just so I can obtain bathroom sex.

A List of Things I Wore When I Was Femme

(non exhaustive)

- my dead grandmother's lipstick (pearly pink, stolen at her wake)

- high-heeled black leather boots I found on the street (for gallery openings)

- orange leather snakeskin patterned tote bag (also found on the street on Capitol Hill)

- sheer, flowered maxi dress (from an upscale consignment boutique)

- glitter on my eyelids (I still do this sometimes, though it is often accompanied by a matching mustache)

- "tomboy femme" t-shirt (gifted to me by Zora)

- a long bob and bangs (accentuated my natural curls)

- my ex-boyfriend's neon yellow cat sweatshirt (purchased on the street in New York)

- countless Victoria's Secret bodysuits (I still wear some of these for drag parties)

- a vintage indigo wrap dress (good for my ass, flexible for nights out or skateboard attempts)

- cat-eye sunglasses (fast-fashion purchase)

- my gold claddagh ring with the heart facing toward me (indicating it is taken; still do this)

- my heart on my sleeve

To ▓▓▓

The worst part is that I dream about you almost every night. In most of the dreams we fight but in some of them we get back together. Even in those ones it isn't the same and I wake up feeling feverish and alone. It's hard because I went through all the emotions of loss when i was at home and now they're all hitting me again at school. Some of the anger has subsided into sadness, but a lot of it is still here which makes the sadness easier to deal with. You haven't responded to any of the times I tried to contact you, which sort of makes sense since most of them were not very pleasant. I still wish you had responded because by ignoring me and cutting me out you made me feel like less of a person. i wonder if we will ever speak to each other again. I wonder if I'll go home for Christmas since you might be there and it'll be too hard knowing you're so close — I'll want to see you or kill you or yell at you or I'll just sit in my bed and cry. We haven't spoken in a couple of weeks, which my mom thinks is good but it hurts. It'll be my first adult Christmas without you. And my birthday. And your birthday. And our old anniversary. And springtime and summer. I called you but you didn't pick up. I think about death a lot. I'm not saying that to be coercive or pitiful, it's just something I thought I was done with. And now I'm not. I'm vulnerable and lonely in a way I haven't been in a long time. But I've been really strong. I haven't cut myself despite how much I want to. I wish I could open my skin and let all the feelings of

15

Small writing. My handwriting has changed. The way I look at the world has changed. Most days I feel shattered by the way that all my fears conspired together to come true — of men, of you, of lies, of cheating, of loneliness, of desperation, of abandonment, of love disappearing. Some days I feel small parts of myself coming back to me, but right now those things are still so very small. Mostly I want to sleep all the time. I want to fast-forward months and years to when it doesn't hurt so crushingly bad anymore. I'm running out of things to say that aren't angry, blameful, hateful, scornful, depressing. You probably won't read this but even if you did I don't think you'd reply. I don't know if I'm writing to you or to me. I wish you hadn't rushed to fill in the space I took up.

I feel empty but my hope is that I'll feel a little less every day - cry a little less, scream into my pillow a little less, stay in bed a little less. I wish for both of us that you had taken the time to reacquaint yourself with me, because I am new and different in so many ways. I worked so hard on myself while I was away, and I came back stronger than I ever was. You definitely set me back in that way, but I'm trying to hold on to who I'm becoming. Maybe one day there will be room for you again. I'm out of energy now.

Not sure how to sign off. You know who it's from.

Leighan

photo of Mort and me by a dear friend, summer 2013

II. Fuck You (A Drawing by Mort)

Let me tell you about my first and only boyfriend, Mort.

He's the one who did the drawing of the many-nippled dog, and the lunchbox that says "LAUNCH." He made it for me, in my sketchbook. I'm not sure why.

The batshit crazy thing about this story is that I'm gay. And we broke up because I was gay. And I blamed him anyway.

Mort and I met in the third grade. He was a chubby kid with a penchant for drawing skateboards, and I was spanking new to Ohio with a penchant for drawing dragons. He and his best friend teased me mercilessly, calling me Scummy Scully. I was totally into the best friend, though. You might be wondering whether a third-grader was capable of being *totally into* someone, but I was. I kept lists in my journal about the features that made him "hot": his big brown eyes, his spiky skater hair. Eating up teenaged books, at the time, as the precocious reader I was, my language was already a bit sexualized.

Mort was less appealing to me. I privately made up mean nicknames to call him back but was far too shy to verbalize them. The ironic thing about the Scummy Scully nickname is that even in childhood, I had severe OCD and cleaned myself compulsively. I was pretty much the opposite of Scummy. Mort didn't care.

In eighth grade, Mort was struck by a car while skateboarding and had some kind of bulky boot on his leg. He was fine, and I laughed. I felt that Mort's skateboarding accident was retribution for the bullying days five years earlier. In truth, I was just being a little shit. In ninth grade, Mort and I both joined the marching band, me on flute and him on percussion. The first time I noticed Mort *like that* was when a pretty, blonde cheer squad member took interest in him. I had always liked boys, and Mort sure was a boy. By tenth grade, I was telling my friends, "If Mort lost like twenty more pounds, I would *totally* fuck him." My juvenile cruelty aside, I also had never fucked anyone. But I was desperate to do so.

A HEALTHY EXCERSISE

FUCK YOU

FUCK YOU

FUCK YOU

FUCK YOU

FUCK YOU

Our first kiss was a tongue-jumble on a bench, in the park nestled between the residential streets of our shared neighborhood. My first real kiss ever, I was sixteen. The pedophile history teacher walked by and watched. Mort asked me to be his girlfriend, and I asked him why we couldn't just hook up. By tenth grade, I was already a commitment-phobe.

But Mort hung out on my basement futon and lifted up my peasant tops and kissed my stomach. I decided to give him an honest-to-God shot. That summer we spent making out everywhere we could, and by the time eleventh grade came around, I was smitten. And by smitten, I mean dependent. It started out sexually. I'd been unbearably horny for my entire fucking life and now I finally had someone who wanted to go down on me? Count me in.

Mort got his license right away and picked me up in his red Toyota. We did a lot of doggie-style in the back of the car, at the town lake or in the driveway of the private girls' school. *Fucking lesbians aren't doing this,* I thought as I was bent over the backseat. None of my friends had boyfriends besides me, so I started talking to the popular girls because they were the only ones who were also having sex. We discussed birth control in Art and side effects in Spanish, and I felt accepted for the first time. Sex, inexplicably, equaled friends.

I became dependent on Mort driving me everywhere. Cursed with a minor knee injury and an anxiety disorder, I didn't get my license until college. Even though we both lived walking distance to school, Mort picked me up every morning so we could walk into class together. He brought me to appointments and alleviated some stress on my parents, who had three kids to shepherd around. He also drove us to his house on our lunch break so we could fuck in his attic bedroom. Sometimes we did this twice a day, during lunch before Spanish, and again during the free period at the end of the day, before our sports teams convened.

Deep into an undiagnosed eating disorder, I relied on Mort for validation about my body, and he did the same through me. We shared in this dysmorphia, running together, encouraging each other to eat "healthy," as I encouraged both of us to stay thin. We fucked, we skipped meals, we made art, we skipped class, we skipped class to fuck, we fucked some more. Our Homecoming photos say it all: his hand wrapped possessively around my waist, my collarbones protruding, both of our cheeks just ever-so-slightly sunken beneath our matching blue eyes. I thought he was the best thing that ever happened to me.

Fast forward to the end of high school. We'd now been together two years, and despite having a more or less mutual agreement to see "how things went" between the start of our freshman year of college and our first winter break, I was more attached than ever. Mort later told me that we should have ended things there, that he already wanted out. Me, I puked in my mouth the entire ride from Cleveland to DC, thinking about living without him. At this point, I had favored our artistic connection, our collaborative nature, our sexual endurance, and our quiet companionship over relationships with my friends. When I had a big falling out with a rowing teammate my senior year, I turned to him to get me through the feelings of regret and isolation. When I drunkenly kissed my closest girl friend at a party, he drove us both home and made sure we got to bed safely. I didn't want anyone but him.

Or so I thought.

Interlude for a Brief Art Historico-Personal Analysis of Mort's Many-Nippled Dog

Mort was most inspired by male artists making work about mundanity. I once asked him what he, Mort, even had to make art about as a white man from an upper middle-class family. We were on a fast train in England, where I was studying abroad, and I rubbed his art in his face. He'd been working for months on a comic called "Average Joe," about, you guessed it, a guy who is painfully and comically average in every way. What I failed to see at the time was that Mort's comic was actually quite ironic, juxtaposing a personal history of a boring man with my boyfriend's unusually skillful illustrations and beautifully rendered script. Mort loved Harvey Pekar, a local Cleveland artist who detailed his life through almost grotesquely honest comics. Actually, Mort's first tattoo was a Pekar panel, reading, "When I was sixteen I discovered jazz records." Mort loved jazz and judged me incessantly for rejecting music without lyrics. (All these years later, I agree with him).

The summer after we turned eighteen, we went to the dinky tattoo shop in the old hippie village, and he got his Pekar tattoo and I got a shamrock on my ribcage. I distinctly remember us fucking on the floor of my sophomore year dorm room while my roommates were out, the tattoo lines of his upper arm muscle colliding with the side of my torso, my lucky shamrock.

Mort also loved Robert Crumb, who made definitively crude, stylistic comics of large, muscled women crushing unassuming, mediocre men. This I could get behind, though part of me felt embarrassed. As an emaciated teenager, I was hardly an intimidating, heavy-lifting man-eater. When I looked at the drawings in Mort's sketchbook of women with heavy breasts or posed sumptuously with their curves emanating from the ink, I felt self-conscious. Did Mort expect me to be like these women? Heck, had Mort ever experienced women like this, whether in dreams or reality? Was that what he wanted? I didn't know.

Let's bring it back to the many-nippled dog. Mort and I both loved dogs and drew them often. I wonder now if he made this drawing for me because of that shared affection, but I also wonder about the palpable *motherness* of the dog, her eight nipples and bared teeth. She reminds me of the women in the Robert Crumb drawings, fecund and physical, a walking confrontation between femininity and fear. When I look at the dog now, I assume she is pregnant. Looking back, I recall a couple of late periods around that time and a lot of anxiety around contraception and pregnancy for me. I had always been nervous around pregnant women and being sexually active as a teenager, surrounded by a load of virgins and some abstinence-first based sex education in school, I was constantly terrified by my anatomy and its potential. Mort and I used to get into fights when I would demand that we have an emergency action plan should my birth control fail. He thought I was stressing about the hypothetical; I thought I was being responsible. I think there was definitely a little of both: on one hand, I *was* a hyper-responsible teenager and that extended to sexual precautions, on the other hand, I had rampant, undiagnosed OCD which manifested in a lot of hypothetical health anxieties.

Now, though, when I look at this picture, I see the dog's shadow.

I almost thought the shadow was a second, tiny, dark dog, but at this time I understand it to be the miniscule shadow of a pregnant dog who has in fact been *launched* into the air, just like the lunchbox says. I like the anonymity of the shadow-dog; I like how it could almost be the future puppy beside its mother. Almost.

III. Thanks, Debbie

girls are always
born too good
girls are never
really born
at all

The first time I saw Veil I thought I had been electrocuted. *Did I just stick my finger into a fucking socket?*

It was the summer after my sophomore year of college, and I was back in my hometown interning at a small art gallery, my relationship with Mort seemingly going strong, though I later learned otherwise.

If I was the fumbly but overcommitted intern those sticky days of June, Veil was the grumpy yet dashing gallery handyman. My supervisor introduced them by their old name, saying, "She helps out around here." I instantly concocted ways to solicit their help.

Sitting at the computer, I asked them for assistance in making some sort of time lapse promo video for the gallery. They put their hand over my hand on the mouse and the electrocution feeling came back in full force. I felt *buzzed.* I tasted strawberries in my mouth and saw stars in my eyes and breathed in their must and knew I had to do something. Mort who?

When my shift at the gallery ended that first day of knowing Veil, I walked out with them. They pushed their bike, and I tried to adjust my pink cropped sweater and long red curls in a way that made me seem like I fucked people besides boys. I said I had to head down the hill and across the bridge to my paying job, coaching adult rowers on the Cuyahoga River, coxing them to win races and coaxing them to buy me a burger afterward. Veil looked down as they agreed to walk me to the boathouse. I can't remember a single thing we spoke of that day, only the exploding feeling inside me that I had just met someone who would leave a mark on my life for-fucking-ever. I didn't believe in love at first sight until that day.

When Mort dutifully picked me up from my shift on the water, I had something to say. "I think, um, I met the love of my life today."

What the fuck? was the reaction in his eyes. I can't remember what he said back to me. Kind of goes to show where my head was at. He probably drove me back to his house where his mom had prepared a delicious family dinner, and we probably fucked it out in the attic after I recounted my shame. I don't remember our relationship feeling particularly threatened, after all, Veil was a "girl."

But threatened it was. Veil and I exchanged numbers and began texting, ostensibly about the gallery, but soon we were full-on getting to know each other. Shy during the gallery days and emboldened behind a screen, I devoured information about them and relished in the fact that a bona fide dyke was giving me the time of day. At the time, I was struggling with defining my own sexuality, but settled into the frequent rumors that I was bisexual. I had kissed girls before, sure, and even had a crush on a couple of the academic lesbians I met at school, but underneath the initial, bubbly excitement of those feelings always came a sinking pit of disappointment in my stomach. I had a loving boyfriend; I didn't *need* to be gay.

I knew Veil was gay, of course, and not just because they dressed "alternative" like some of the theater kids I went to high school with: ripped jeans, homemade shirts, colorful sneakers with rainbow laces and fading green hair dye washing over their naturally brown-black curls. Two bright tattoo sleeves featuring women saints and their friends' names. They just had this queer magnetism about them. When I looked at them, I felt as though someone had planted a bed of flowers at the bottom of the pit in my stomach, watering them incessantly as they sprang up, threatening to grow out of my throat and explode out of my mouth. A floral vomit is what I felt when I looked at Veil. They reminded me of some of the butch lesbians in my women's studies classes, one of whom I harbored a secret crush on the semester before, but somehow *more.* They were the gayest thing I had ever seen.

Our first date was an accident. It happened because the other intern, Debbie, told us to go on ahead without her. We had a gallery lunch break at the same time, and Veil walked with me to the hipster tea shop in the artsy (gentrified) industrial neighborhood nearby. I probably ordered something high maintenance, and they probably ordered the closest thing to black coffee the shop had. We just sipped our iced drinks and talked, laughing about the other interns and how they probably thought we were on a date. Maybe a little astrology thrown in there, we were both earth signs, after all. When we came back, I knew for sure I was smitten. Later we would joke, "Thanks, Debbie."

The summer days dragged on, but the season unfurled as quickly as the flowers growing in my stomach. I worked at the gallery by day and coached the boats in the evenings. Mort painted houses and worked on his comic project. I came home to Mort and his mother's prepared dinners, and we had sweaty attic sex when I took off his white painter's overalls. Veil and I followed each other on Instagram, and I quietly lusted after their punk selfies and protest pictures. Things came to a head over text the day gay marriage was legalized.

On June 26th, 2015, I typed out a message asking them to kiss. Or maybe they asked me. All I know is that suddenly, we were arranging to meet outside of work, and I talked Mort into giving me a ride. He dropped me off outside Veil's mom's house that dark, hot evening, I'm sure with an I Love You, and then drove away. I was exhilarated with a fickle sense of freedom as I walked onto the porch, dimly lit by a green bulb that always made me think of a Van Gogh painting. When Veil came out to meet me, the ethics of what I was doing or how Mort must've been feeling escaped me. My mind was blank with happiness.

Veil walked me to the dam where the high school kids went to do drugs. I'd never been. This was pretty out of character for me; I'd always been a bit of a prissy rule-follower. Sure, I smoked and I drank and went to parties at school, but I'd never seen this gritty, punk underside of my hometown. After we scooted down to the water through all the graffitied rocks, I sat next to Veil and started talking. We talked for hours, some of it flirting, some of it heavy, like about how Veil's roommate had shot herself in the head earlier that summer. At some late hour, it started to rain, and we started to kiss.

It wasn't just any kiss. I pulled off my college sweatshirt and sat shivering in my black tanktop. I put each of my legs over Veil's thighs, facing them in a kind of frog-sitting-on-a-lap position. I kissed them mercilessly, and they kissed me back the same way. Our bodies gyrated toward each other, our hips moving in rhythm, our pelvises nearly touching. The rain wet my long hair, and I breathed Veil in. They smelled like cigarettes and black coffee and a little bit of earth, and I thought, "this is being gay." Remember that electrified feeling I had when I saw them for the first time? That was nothing compared to this. Now, I felt like I was taking a bath with a hair dryer and I never wanted the goosebumps to go down.

We kissed for ages. In the early hours of the morning, damp with rain and sweat, Veil walked me home. It was a long walk, and they held my hand the whole way. My fingers felt like starlight and my lips blushed violently. Their deep brown eyes glittered in the dark like the mouths of caves. I kissed them goodnight on my parent's doorstep and fell into a blissfully dreamless sleep. I would deal with Mort in the morning.

I found this in my journal from the next day:

IV. I'm So Miserable Without You It's Almost Like Having You Here

Things fell apart with Mort one morning in July. He was in New York for the summer, and I was in Cleveland with Veil. It was the summer before my senior year of college. Mort had some new friends he'd been hanging out with whom I hadn't met, some skaters and artists and a girl named Trina. I did my usual hot day routine of rolling out of Veil's bed at the guitar studio where they lived, ready to walk home and get ready to work at the boathouse that evening. I loved leaving the guitar studio in the mornings. I'd taken lessons there as a kid, and now that I was all grown up, I could leave my lover's bed at my leisure, wearing their clothes, walking the many blocks home covered in their spit. They had this one shirt from their uncle that I liked especially, it was a bright teal green and in white lettering read, I'm So Miserable Without You It's Almost Like Having You Here. I wore it all the time. In fact, I was wearing it on this particular morning in July.

I was texting Mort on my way home as I often did, smiling my big smile of *holy shit I have two lovers I'm the luckiest bitch in the world.* I dropped the smile pretty fast. "I need to tell you that I hooked up with Trina last night," Mort messaged. I think I answered, "What the fuck?" I immediately felt the vomit creeping up in my throat, not floral but rancid, like if the flowers were rotten.

I was supposed to be taking the bus from Cleveland to Chicago the following morning to visit a college friend. I spent the afternoon crying as I packed, my mother not understanding why I was so upset with Mort, since I was also dating Veil. Looking back, it makes sense that my mom was confused: wasn't I holding Mort to a double standard? How come I could have a whole other partner, but he wasn't allowed to hook up with a girl in New York? I passed it off as her inability to process the nuances of polyamory, but she was on to a pattern that would repeat throughout my dating life: I want my cake and I want to eat it, too.

30

I often use the old non monogamous verbiage to support my desires: equity, not equality. Meaning, both partners don't need to act exactly the same in a relationship, but each should honor the agreements they have made together. But in truth, my inner dialogue didn't give a shit about equity. In fact, I have often used this polyamorous proverb to justify my manipulative or unfair behavior. One thing about me is that I can *always* justify why I'm right and my partner is wrong. It's almost like a talent.

How was this not Mort cheating on me? Before I pursued Veil, I had communicated with him as extensively as I could, and he had vehemently denied anything going on between him and Trina. I felt lied to. In my self-righteous head, I was allowed Veil, but Mort wasn't allowed Trina because I had let him know ahead of time that I was going to fuck someone else, not after the fact. In my defense, we were definitely not on the same page, and as far as nonmonogamy goes, that's really not cool. The day the previous summer Mort and I had picked up a pizza for a picnic by the little lake, me wearing his oversized neon cartoon sweatshirt, he was gently crying as I professed my attraction to Veil. Whatever, I'd thought. Fuck this guy.

I was defensive with my mom. My parents had been nonchalant when I came out as queer, a little surprised due to the obvious "red herring," as my mom called Mort later. When I came out as polyamorous, though, shit hit the fan. I never felt guiltier about seeing Veil more than when I told my mom. Playing devil's advocate in defense of Mort, a boy she had grown to love as part of the family, it was as if I'd wounded her as well. When I first told her about Veil, I was lying in bed when she came into my room.

"Mom," I said sheepishly, "I have to tell you about something that's going on."

She raised her eyebrows with a suspicious British, "Hmmmm?"

"I've been hooking up with this girl."

"What? What does that mean? What about Mort?"

"Just like, kissing and stuff. Mort knows."

"I don't want any sex stuff happening in my house."

We had several fights about the whole thing after that. I think I had more fights with my mom about polyamory that first summer of Veil than I did with Mort. Maybe, therein lies the problem.

One year later, on this beautiful July day, my mom tried to comfort me as best she could while trying to hide her exasperation. I didn't try to hide mine.

On my way to Chicago, I interrogated Mort via text while I cried on the bus. I needed to know every detail. I needed to get it out of him. I needed to know exactly which sex acts he had performed on Trina. I needed to know how badly he had fucked up. He was resistant at first, and then he gave up the information I was looking for. I'm sure that made us both feel worse. I remember saying to him, "You could have communicated. You could have had both of us and now you can have neither of us." Presumptuous of me to assume that he would leave things alone with Trina based on my feelings alone.

When I arrived at my friend's house in a gated suburban community with a pool, I decided to retaliate. While ignoring Mort's texts, I posted an Instagram of me looking very hot on a pool float, sliding my sunglasses down with my finger to look at the camera. The caption read: *When you were too hot for him anyway.* We broke up.

Veil picked up the pieces that summer, or tried to. They were picking up the pieces for quite a long time. I spent the majority of my free time senior year of college in therapy, crying about the betrayal of Mort. Veil made themselves available, supported me through my mournful seasons, and cheered me on until graduation. Veil's big moment was coming to the graduation ceremony, an occasion I had always pictured experiencing with Mort. But there we were, me, my parents, my aunt, and Veil at the fancy restaurant that evening.

Earlier on graduation day, my roommates and I marched down to the National Mall in our precarious heels, smiling and feeling extra petty toward our collective ex-boyfriends. *Fuck em, we look hot.* Veil met me on the mall wearing their long hair in a ponytail and their favorite sweater of mine, something distinctly Ron Weasley-looking. I always loved when they dressed up. Nothing could foil this happiness! I had worked hard for four years, both academically and at several jobs, earning spending money, and I was ready for this new phase working at the H Street art gallery and being with Veil, the love of my life.

All went as planned except for the ducklings. There were always ducklings in the reflecting pools of the National Mall, tourists cooing at their cuteness, kids desperately trying to pet them by offering breadcrumbs in outstretched hands. The thing is, all the ducklings were dead that day. I mean every fucking one of them. We had to take pictures with our backs blocking out the little waves of dead ducklings floating by in the background. Someone told us, the horrified new graduates, that there was something in the water that day, poisonous algae or some shit, that it was toxic to the little birds. I tried my best not to think of it as an omen, but I did. And maybe it was.

A few months later, in September, Veil and I took a long trip to Northern California to visit their much-older half-sister and niece. I had never been more in love. We traversed the cliff bluffs, picked out oblong stones for our future wedding rings at the beach full of sea glass, fucked deliciously while we imagined our life together in this beautiful place. As I held hands with Veil's little niece crossing the rainbow streets of Oakland, I pictured us having kids. I read lesbian poetry aloud to Veil in the hilly grass parks of San Francisco. We were blissed the fuck out.

The little fights started after that. I was going through a rough patch: a little aimless straight out of college, working too much for too little pay, falling out with my college friends left and right. The question of whether Veil would move to DC for me loomed above us constantly. They wanted to be with me, but opportunities were arising for them up in Cleveland: they were offered a mural-painting job, and they were going to be in an art show at the community college. One late night at work, I sat outside on the gallery patio talking to them on the phone. I was berating them for not having gotten their shit together and made a final decision yet. They were gently telling me the input that they were getting from their friends and family was making them question why everything had to be about my success, on my timeline. Why couldn't they also do what was best for them? They stood up for themselves. I hated it.

"Veil, fuck your friends, and fuck your family." I spat into the phone that night, surrounded by the pretty twinkling lights of the gallery.

"Baby!" they exclaimed, horrified. I didn't feel bad.

The last time I saw Veil was when I went up to Cleveland for their art show. I was so proud of them. We both wore our best outfits and kissed in front of their huge piece on the wall of the community college. We had a great weekend, but when I got back to DC, shit hit the fan. I started fucking my best friend. Veil started having flashbacks of the fucked up things that happened to them years before meeting me. I was so wrapped up in my own petty shit that I preemptively broke up with them over text. My style has always been to hurt before I can get hurt, and this was no different.

I tried to take it back almost immediately, but Veil was mentally long gone. Not answering my texts or calls. It was over, and I felt my heart break with every fingernail I painted black. I thought about killing myself. Instead, I got a really expensive tattoo, a perfect circle of a line around my right mid-forearm. People kept complimenting it, asking me what it meant. What I didn't tell them was that I got it to keep me from slitting my wrist.

The I'm So Miserable Without You shirt still sits in my closet to this day. It's faded from too many washes, trying to get their smell out of it. I thought about burning it, the beacon of the breakups of my two most significant relationships, but I haven't been able to bring myself to do it. I tried to sell it, but no one wanted it. I was going to donate it but I didn't want some unsuspecting person to pick up a silly shirt, offhandedly, with seriously cursed energy. So, in my closet it sits.

Archived Posts on Instagram: A Reckoning

February 14th, 2018:

sometimes a picture says what words can't / to my love who I can't be with today: thank you for showing me that love isn't pointless, isn't selfish, isn't too good for me. you're my partner, my muse, my catalyst for realizing who I really am in many ways. i celebrate you every day.

October 8th, 2018:

beautiful boy.

January 27th, 2019:

my heart: *is beating for masc women*

July 30th, 2019:

hey you touched my arm twice during your serenade last night lmk if you want to fuck sometime

August 18th, 2019:

late summer lesbian weekend: breakup ceremony & group sex auditions & advocacy brunch for dykes getting free sperm

December 19th, 2019:

a year ago today i saw them for the first time / they were performing I was with my girlfriend / wearing a pink dress for my birthday / I don't wear dresses anymore and tonight they did a show just for me

V. I Love You But I'm Not In Love With You

The first thing I ever said to Fern was, "You are a vision." Honestly, to this day I still think it was a pretty strong opening line, and I'm less embarrassed than I should be that I have used it since on several other people. But Fern was the person for whom I *meant it.* Yeah, my slick line was over Tinder, but hey, it got their attention.

Fern and I talked a lot before we ever met up. This wasn't really my style, but they were a farmer a couple hours north of me in New Hampshire, and a same-night sexual tryst was not in the cards. So, we talked. Or rather, they asked me a lot of personal questions and I sexualized the conversation. I pretty much always do that. Someone wants to talk to me about music or poetry and I tell them that I'm not wearing underwear. But Fern was a vision. So, I persevered.

Hampton Beach on the New Hampshire coastline was set as the location of our highly anticipated meetup, a couple weeks into talking daily. Rita drove me up from Boston and generously waited in the car while I went to greet Fern in the beach parking lot. The first thing they noticed about me in the flesh was my frenulum piercing, usually referred to as a smiley. It's usually only visible when I do a big smile with all my teeth, and that is certainly what I was doing as Fern walked over to me that first day. Tall, well-muscled, with curly brown hair and hazel eyes, I was immediately taken with them. I knew they worked hard farming and I could see it in their physique. Broad shoulders, long legs, big hands. A voice deepened by testosterone shots. A septum piercing which I complemented back. A virtual vision come to life.

Fern smiled a lot, too. A lot more than me, actually, noticeably so. On the beach, we walked and put our feet in the frigid February water, eventually settling down on some rocks where we huddled together for warmth. Both of us were complaining about our nearly-blue fingers at this point, so we held hands. Fern told me that they loved eye contact more than anything and that I was good at it. I blushed because usually I freak people out with my unbroken gaze, especially when I'm attracted to someone. Fern loved it. We must have sat for at least thirty minutes, freezing wind whipping around us, hands entwined, eyes wide and staring into each other's pupils. I thought their name must be Fern because of the mossy color of their eyes, but it wasn't.

After a while on the beach, I had stared at Fern's face for so long that it started morphing into strange shapes. I never wear my glasses on first dates, and my eyes have trouble focusing on two things together at the same time. Fern had this almost moony look in their eyes, their face permanently lit up with a smile, a lock of their hair falling forward charmingly. I started to grow a little disturbed by the face shapes I was seeing, of the wind skating over the sand in my peripheral, of the way Fern seemed content to do this forever. Their face blurred because I was so close to it. I asked if I could kiss their cheek. Then I asked if I could kiss their lips.

Making out with Fern stirred something up inside me. I hadn't kissed anyone since my last breakup a few months earlier, and I was feeling pretty dead to the world physically. I mean, I am a sex addict. You ever tried being a sex addict with no sex for more than a week? It's no good, take it from me. So, the kiss was passionate. So passionate that I lost track of time and had missed several ARE U ALIVE texts from Rita while the chilly world stopped around us. I assured Rita I was okay while Fern took their clothes off, right there on the beach. *Aren't you getting in the water?*

They ran into the waves, muscles rippling across their back, diving into the late February foam. When they came out, we kissed some more and ran to their car to warm up, just across the parking lot from where Rita was playing a virtual design game on her phone. We had sex then, tugging at each other's damp coats and putting the seats down as quickly as we could while trying not to remove our hands from each other's bodies. Theirs was salty. It was dark at this point, so I invited them into Rita's backseat for introductions before we whizzed off home to Boston so I could warm up. Fern kissed me in front of Rita and left. A few hours later they would tell me that they listened to Perfume Genius's *Set My Heart On Fire Immediately* album the whole way home. That night I started a playlist for them and wanted to call it "Hampton Beach Kisses" but thought that was too mushy and decided against it. Instead, I sent them three hours of love songs, thinking I was being tactful.

Things with Fern ran fast and hot. Pretty soon, they were driving the three hours round trip to see me for one night a weekend, which wasn't exactly sustainable on a farmer's schedule. Fern often woke up long before the sun, went for a run through the woods, bathed in the stream near their mother's house, and hauled ass at the farm all day. Farmers don't really get days off, but at this point, they were part-time between the farm and the local market, leaving them free for me for approximately eighteen hours at a time.

This one-night-a-week-rendezvous-across-state-lines thing burnt out pretty quickly. I liked the idea of fucking a farmer, (what strong fingers!) but I hated having to wait to see them. My codependent tendencies made it so that I wanted to be with someone all. the. time. Fern couldn't give that to me, but in the days apart they sent me poems, songs, and words of affirmation. Eventually they asked me to take the bus up to their mother's house to visit them, which I did precisely twice.

The first time I visited the small New Hampshire town that hardly had a center, there was a conflict of interest. Fern wanted to show me their hiking spots, their swimming spots, their running spots, to be outside with me. I wanted to stay in their bed the entire time. As things generally go, I got my way. We fucked everywhere. In the car, in the shower, on the floor, in the woods, on the banks of the pond near their house, in the cemetery where I sat on their face and felt the sun on my shoulders. Fern's mother later commented to them, *My, don't you spend a lot of time in your bedroom.* I wasn't ashamed. I was thrilled that this beautiful country boy twink wanted to go down on me for hours, and I hardly let them up for air. Give me a tall brunette and I become bed-bound.

When we trespassed at a local boat club, we stripped to our underwear and dived off the dock into the cool April water. Fern looked beautiful with water dripping from their brow. We had said *I Love You* before that, lying in a field of daffodils at the Arnold Arboretum, but there on the dock, lying in the crook of Fern's arm, I said *I Love You So Much.* I could feel Fern nuzzle me with acknowledgment and I waited for them to reciprocate the sentiment. They did not.

Walking back down the dusty road of the boat club, I started to cry. Teenage boys jogged past us, jostling each other raucously, and I worried about the homophobic shit they might say until I remembered that Fern passed as a boy. Fern held my hand but didn't ask me why I was crying. Fern asked me a lot of questions, but never about why I was crying. I broached my own sadness aloud.

"Why can't you just say that you love me SO MUCH too?" I wailed. Fern frowned, as they often did while I cried, and told me that this kind of a thing was reserved for their mother, their best friend. I couldn't accept this answer, so I pushed.

"I love you, but I'm not *in* love with you yet."

Fern explained that their love timeline looked a little differently than mine. I was distraught. How could I be with someone who wasn't already madly in love with me? I cried the entire way they drove me to the bus station and sent them a bitchy text when I got home, for good measure.

That was the last time I saw Fern. The following week they FaceTimed me and let me talk for close to an hour, nervously rambling about the small frustrations of my day before they said, "Baby, I don't think we can do this anymore." I cried, I hung up, I called back, I sent more bitchy texts.

"I thought you were calling to tell me everything was going to be alright," I sobbed. This got them, tears flowing down their pixelated face. Fern explained that their time at the farm was ramping up for the summer season, that they didn't have the energy to keep driving to see me. I knew this was reasonable, but I refused to concede, even though a few days prior I had described myself as *miserable in this relationship* to my sister on the phone. I decided I was interested in killing myself and flew home to Ohio.

It was there in my mother's garden that I realized I might have a little bit of a problem with this whole love thing.

Selections from the Would-Be *Hampton Beach Kisses* Playlist

- Make Out in My Car, Moses Sumney
- Andromeda, Weyes Blood
- Nothing's Gonna Hurt You Baby, Cigarettes After Sex
- Walden Pond, Atta Boy
- Blue Sky and Yellow Sunflower, Susumu Yokota
- You Can Have It All, Yo La Tengo
- Cherry Wine, Overcoats
- Shark Smile, Big Thief
- I Think You're Alright, Jay Som
- Your Body Changes Everything, Perfume Genius

VI. Don't Call Me That

Em and I first slept together the day after I returned from a camping trip from the Cape. She came over wearing those expensive white sneakers, which I hated, her hair a little too neatly cut. My online dating profile said something along the lines of, "Looking for a butch rebound." She messaged right away as Rita drove us home from camping, affirming that she was both butch and seeking a rebound as well.

In the flesh, she kind of seemed like one of those girls who really had to work at being butch, her energy didn't feel particularly masculine, but she was tall, so I opened the door. We shared a joint on my back porch and swapped biphobic comments, though hers felt worse than mine since she was a Gold Star lesbian, meaning she'd never been with a man. I obviously had, five formative years with Mort under my belt, which shocked Em since I seemed so gay. I said, "Doesn't that make me *more* gay? That I was with a man and then *chose* to commit my life to lesbianism?" She didn't seem to think so.

I knew we were going to fuck even though she declined to answer my question the night before we met up, the one about what her lingerie color preferences were. I thought this made her awkward. Turns out, I was right, and she would never be good at dirty talk. The sex was decent, though I had to encourage her to go harder, that she wouldn't hurt me, that maybe I liked being hurt. This was apparently not her jam, so we ended up having what I call "lovey sex" for the next ten months. Which isn't exactly my jam. But I didn't want to be alone for the winter.

When we were finished that first night in early July, I rolled over and asked whether she developed feelings easily. She gave a nervous non-answer which I took to mean yes, and I explained that I most certainly do not. Which meant unless it suits me.

We had a little back and forth over the following weeks, her texting me that she'd love to see me and me mostly blowing her off except when I was bored. This was a point of contention for our entire relationship: that I was being a fuckboy (again) at the beginning, that I didn't want to see her as much as she wanted to see me. I presumed the reason she wanted to hang out was because I was good at sex, but I prefer to slow things down after what probably should've been a one-night stand. I think it's because I like fucking on my first meeting with someone, get any nerves out of the way, you know? But then the mystery's gone. Plus, I'm a top, so my arm tends to get sore. After that initial romp, I like to see what I think of this person on the whole, hang out as friends, maybe make out a bit to see if there's actually chemistry there, or not if it turned out I was just high in the dark the other night.

After a couple weeks of this, I went to a neighborhood yard sale for a friend who was moving to Chicago. All of her roommates were there, including one who caught my eye immediately. Their name was Paulie and they were gangly and brunette and wearing a backwards baseball cap. I licked my lips without meaning to. Paulie and I started talking, and it turned out they were moving too but staying within the neighborhood. I asked where, and they said that group house on Walnut. "Holy shit, I think I know one of your future roommates," I replied, cursing my luck. Paulie demanded to know who, and I gave it up quickly: it was Em.

"Oh really? That's funny. How do you know Em? I haven't even met her yet."

"We're sleeping together."

"Of course."

The following Saturday was my friend's going away party, and I knew Paulie would be there, so I wore a zip up bodysuit and a leather collar. Frankly, I followed Paulie around the whole night like a sick puppy, totally blowing my cover, but the heart(?) wants what it wants.

Eventually, the guests cleared out and I was still there. Paulie offered to give me a ride home so I wouldn't be walking back up the hill to my place in the early hours of the morning. It wasn't long before they pulled over to unzip my bodysuit. We had a steamy and euphoric time in the car, my hand pressed against the window a la that stupid Titanic scene. I was thrilled when they dropped me off. Then I remembered Em. Shit.

The next day, I sent some bullshit cryptic text along the lines of *we need to talk.* I would have hated to get a text like that. She responded right away, "Can you say more about what you'd like to talk to me about?"

"Paulie and I hooked up last night."

Long pause. An agreement to meet in person to talk. Some light crying on her part. A text from Paulie while she was over. She asked, "Is that them now?" I said yes and that I was going over to their place after she left. More crying. I quoted a stupid meme to her, "You're so pretty ahahaha, don't cry," and then walked her to the door before putting on something sexy and butch and setting off for the hill up to Paulie's soon-to-be-old house.

Paulie opened the door to their basement room, and I explained quickly that I had talked to Em so it was all good for us to fuck. We got into bed, and I noticed for the first time how Paulie gawked. They pulled their packer out of their underwear, and I carefully avoided the tape on their chest. The sex was nothing special, the two of us voraciously going at it in the hope of feeling something. When they were done, they got up and told me they had something they wanted to show me. I thought this was kind of sweet and sat up on the bed in anticipation. Paulie turned around then and whacked me with a pool noodle that seemed to be disguised as a lightsaber. I was horrified. They laughed and ate some of those little chocolate cube cookies in their bed before inviting me upstairs to microwave taquitos. It was like fucking a college boy. I hated it.

Shortly after Paulie and I consummated our non-relationship, I set off to visit my sister in France, where I would meet with another lover for the first time in a year. At this point, I had let Em know that the Paulie thing was *so* not happening, and she obediently returned to my bed. I kissed her goodbye before my flight and decided to ghost her newly-minted roommate, Paulie. After we'd hooked up, my body felt sick for weeks. And not in a sexy yearning way. In a way that there was something wrong. I felt uncomfortable, unseen. I felt that Paulie had just used me to get off and then hit me with that fucking noodle. I felt objectified. Em agreed that she hated them too and would ignore them around the Walnut Street house. I went to Paris with Em wrapped around my finger.

Less than six months later, Em and I adopted a puppy together. We'd had a fair amount of practice dog sitting for a weirdo pair called Frankie and Clara, a chiweenie and cattle dog mix respectively. The first time Em and I fucked after I got home from Paris was in the dog sitting house. I'd been mourning leaving my lover overseas and couldn't bring myself to be intimate with another person. That night at the dogs' house, though, we were watching *Sex Education*, which, surprise surprise, always makes me horny. We started making out on the couch until things escalated into the bedroom, Frankie and Clara following us, tails wagging.

Em and Clara

I should specify that the puppy we adopted was, in fact, *my* dog, and still is. But I can't pretend that Em and I didn't bring him home as a couple, resistant as I was to putting a label on things with her. When they put the small, black puppy in my arms for the first time at the shelter, I cried while Em took pictures. She drove us the cold hour home with me and the puppy, who I'd already named Vincent, huddling together in the backseat. Every so often she turned around and smiled at me. Within a couple hours, Vincent was sleeping peacefully on Em's chest while I worked remotely. A week to the day that we brought him home, Em posted on her Instagram, "We brought Vincent home a week ago and love him so much already." I'd show you a picture of the post, but I think she blocked me.

Em was openly in love with me at this point, a sentiment I hadn't returned but demanded to hear out loud during sex so I could get off. I'd met her parents, and since bringing Vincent home, she'd essentially moved into my house, sleeping with me every night, pitching in for groceries, taking showers with me in the morning. Em told me several times that her mom said we looked so *cozy* together. And we were. Plus, we both hated Paulie, who sulked at Em's house seemingly full-time.

The thing was, Em started to get resentful toward Vincent pretty quickly. A chronic people pleaser, her entire schtick was doing everything for me before I got around to asking for it or doing it myself, sowing small but perennial seeds of resentment. Em was the one who got up with him in the night and drove him to the vet, because I'm a heavy sleeper and don't have a car. Em was the one who took him out to potty and for walks on snowy nights, because, well, I'm fucking lazy. The crazy thing was, though, that Em never complained about it. She was so happy to sleep in my arms that she would do whatever it took to stay there. If you think I'm painting Em as pathetic here, I promise I'm not. I take full responsibility for being the pathetic one. I mean, I basically crafted a relationship with a live-in mommy/best friend/dog walker, who also wanted to perform oral sex on me constantly. Codependent who?

A few months later, our little family took an ill-fated March vacation to a remote chalet in New Hampshire owned by longtime friends. It should have been perfect: this house in the woods, Em and I in bed together, our friends in the room downstairs, Vincent sleeping peacefully. And parts of it were idyllic: we taught Vincent how to swim and how to run off leash. We drove the long forest-lined highways of the White Mountains listening to John Denver. We dipped in every waterfall's basin in a fifty-mile radius. We took a tiny cog train up Mount Washington wearing matching overalls and kissed in the tundra-like conditions. We had good sex. But something had shifted in me, and I could sense a downward spiral coming.

This was all well and good before the fighting started. It was, shall we say, classic for me to feel really unwell when we were supposed to be having a nice time. And Em was used to that. She dutifully drove the three hours back and forth to Boston several days that week, heading back to the city to work and returning to check on me. Around this time, I decided I maybe was in love with her after all. I mean, who does that for someone?

Liked by **and others**

sorry I said I could never love you lol I take it back big time

It all came crashing down because of a fucking bumper sticker. It was St. Patrick's Day. I have a love/hate relationship with Saint Patrick's Day. I love it because the sober, Boston Irish, little schoolgirl in me used to revel in correcting people that it wasn't St. *Patty's,* but St. *Paddy's,* DUH! I hate it because when I was twenty-four and in the psych ward, the group therapist wore a St. Patrick's Day sweatshirt. She had the whole nine yards: clover earrings, green socks. The picture of spring, withering in an institution room with bars on the windows. She enthusiastically asked us what we were excited for that spring, which I found rather distasteful in a room of adults being held inside against their will. Anyway, the bumper sticker.

The Irish schoolgirl part of me demanded that we drive on a New Hampshire mountain highway to a specialty dog bakery. This is exactly the kind of thing I do all the time: make highly specific requests for spontaneous adventures, which initially everyone finds charming. Then they just think I'm manic. We got to the dog bakery, and Em stayed in the car. I pored over the shelves of treats and pupcakes and toys and buttons that said things like "UNITY" with a cat and dog entwined on them. Kind of disturbing, really.

49

One of my favorite silly facts about Em was that she was a Horse Girl. If you don't know what a Horse Girl is in the context of the queer community, it's basically what it sounds like. It's kind of that niche intersection between rich kids who grow up owning ponies and little freak kids who larp as horses full-time. Em's family owned several horses, and she grew up riding. Once, when we were finished having sex, I asked her to tell me a secret. She said she would tell one if I did. My secret was that I was a closeted Harry Potter fanatic. Her secret was that she was a Horse Girl. So there in the bakery, in all its glory, I saw a pink camouflage bumper sticker that said, "Thank God I'm a Country Girl," with a sparkly horse on it.

Em had recently gotten a new car, a mint green Subaru that would've been hot if it wasn't so *mommy.* In that moment in the specialty dog bakery, I decided this sticker was the be all and end all of humor, hotness, and reclamation of Horse Girl culture. I bought it immediately, literally grinning. When I came back out to the car to see Em and Vincent, I first presented the obligatory shamrock-shaped dog pastry from the open window and announced I had the perfect present for Em. I can only describe what I was feeling as glee. I had done it again! A snarky gift, but my heart was in the right place. This is why everyone thought I was so charming.

"I am NOT putting that on my car," Em said with a straight face. I looked back at the pristine green of Em's bumper. It was so blank. Prime real estate for some character. I frowned. "And why not?"

"Because, people might think I'm like, *conservative.*"

I got in the car silently, my pride in gift-giving as a love language wounded. "You know, Em, you can never just take a joke."

Em made that face that she made a lot, the one which meant she was going to start to cry soon. She did that thing with her hands that indicated exasperation.

"I'm just not putting that stupid sticker on my car. Maybe we can get another one when we get back to Boston. Just not that one." She looked at me, begging me to drop it. I didn't.

"You're so fucking sensitive. It's like walking on eggshells with you all the time."

"It's like walking on eggshells with ME? It's like walking on eggshells with you! And don't tell me I'm sensitive. What am I supposed to say to that?"

In true lesbian form, we both cried. Sitting in the car, with the dog in the back, his puff pastry untouched, the offending sticker sitting between us on the dash like it was spewing smoke. When we got home, we both left the car silently, knowing something was damaged. I pointedly left the pink camo bumper sticker in the glove compartment and carried my dog inside.

Inevitably, a few weeks later, everything went to shit. I had confronted Em on a walk in the arboretum, asking what her problem was with me lately. She cried some more. She cried until I cried, too. She was always crying, it seemed. We discussed the possibility of ending our relationship and later that night, in bed together as always, I told her I was in love with her back. I have no idea if this was true, which probably means that it wasn't. She told me it seemed like I was just telling her this so she wouldn't leave me. I told her I was just telling her this so that if she did leave me, that shouldn't be the reason.

Around this time, the effects of my meds started to plateau. I was thinking more of my bad thoughts, which were further triggered by interpersonal conflict. You can't fight with me: I *will* kill myself. It's so fucking manipulative. Honestly, that feels good to say.

I told Em I wanted to lie down beside her and never wake up. I told her that if I lived, I wanted her to be my girlfriend. She got me on the phone with my family and my psychiatrist. She kissed me goodbye when I left for the airport to go home to my parents. She texted, most days, while I was in Ohio, checking to see how I was doing, and I told her I had a new prescription and was working through things with my therapist. I told her I might get better soon and that I loved her. I was supposed to stay at my parents' for four days, just until I got over the suicide risk hump. I stayed for three weeks.

My communication with Em fell off a little during this time. My therapist helped me craft a text to her now that I had some space and clarity to determine what I wanted to say. I told her I loved her, that I wanted to be with her, that I was sorry for not being well, and that I appreciated everything she had done for me. I think I knew what was coming so I kept pushing my flight back.

The day I finally got on a plane home to Boston, she sent a curt message asking me to talk as soon as I was home. I told her that this stressed me out and that we could talk on the phone in the airport. I have a history of crying on the phone in the Cleveland airport. When she called, I was pissed. Her voice was flat. I used her full name, called her Emily. "Don't call me that," I could hear the hiss in her voice. "You only call me Emily when you're mad." Our call ended shortly after that.

As promised, she came over right after I texted that I got home. We sat in that stupid fucking green Subaru with the unadorned bumper while she told me all the reasons she couldn't be with me. It was a laundry list. I leaned in to kiss her neck, tears streaming down both our faces. She nudged me away with a peck on the cheek, and I knew things were over. I told her people fight. She told me, not like this. "I hope you have a good life, Em."

"I hope you have a good life, too."

"I'll think of you when I'm swimming."

"I'll think of you when I'm swimming, too."

I walked onto the porch and watched her cry in her car. I

went back to the street and waved at her window for one last hug. I thought it would be the last time I saw the mint Subaru, but I was wrong. Shortly afterward, she started hanging out all the time with her coffee shop manager, who lived across the street from me. So instead of parking outside my house, she was one block over in front of hers. I decided I hated her, seeing that car sitting there every day. Someone told me to key it. I didn't, but I do wonder: what kind of person doesn't say goodbye to the dog?

VII. White Walls

Sometimes, when I'm really high, I tell people I dated Dana for her porn star boobs. I know this makes me sound like an absolute fuck, but I've always been a tits guy. And Dana looked like a Greek statue, long legs and perfect curves and high cheekbones. One time, we were making out in a park in Baltimore, and a guy asked us if we were sisters. I should've been grossed out, but instead I was flattered.

I met Dana when she skateboarded into my art gallery job. This won her major points in my mind. She wore skate shoes like Mort used to and had an aloof, slightly effeminate male air to her. That was the day that I was selling zines at a stoop sale in the neighborhood, so I had a bunch of little DIY copy-machine books on hand. I gave Dana the art spiel and tried to play it cool, but as she was leaving to skate up the hill to DC's Union Station to head back to Baltimore, I decided to shoot my shot. I gave her my most precious zine, the one with the love songs. I made sure my Instagram handle was on the back and told her she could hit me up on the internet if she wanted. A couple days later, she did.

I started making up excuses to take the MARC train out of my city and into hers. After we'd been sleeping together for a few weeks, I realized I didn't know her last name. I think it was then that we decided to date, after swimming in the dam with Dana's acrobat friend who was too nice to the policeman telling us off. We were full-on attached at the hip by weekend, calling out of our jobs to sleepover during the week. I took her to a pumpkin patch, and she told me her dad was kind of homophobic but would maybe come to her wedding. Except instead of her wedding, she said "ours." I posted a photo of her gazing at me in the grass. I called her "beautiful boy."

When I think of Dana, I think of her in the bath. The night I dog sat on Capitol Hill and we stayed in an art critic's townhouse with a deep blue tiled tub. I took pictures of her, sitting legs open, mouth open, laughing before I joined her. At this point, her hair had faded from a deep purplish brown back to its normal almost ginger color. We could have been sisters. My roommate once told me, "Hey, if I could fuck myself like that, I would too." I thought Dana was most beautiful in the water, even in her shithole shower where the cat had died.

Dana lived in this kooky warehouse that a number of Baltimore artists and musicians had squatted in over the years. She had a strange cast of roommates: the former stripper who kept rats in a giant cage, the nerdy guy whose girlfriend was a lowkey feminist punk icon. When we found the cat, someone wanted to name him Jake, but that was already one of the roommate's names. So, I called him Cody. Cody slept with us in Dana's loft bed in her nasty room with dirt on the floor and her dead dog's collar on the nightstand. Dresses hung from her ceiling which I not so secretly hoped she never wore, because dresses turn me off. She told me she liked feeling feminine sometimes, that she thought of herself as a gay boy. I scrunched up my face and told her that was gross.

The walls were the best part of that rancid room: completely blank. I filled them with poems, haiku for Dana and little lyrics of love for her to look at on the nights I wasn't there. I could imagine her and Cody, cozy and orbited by my carefully-chosen words, a piece of me always with her.

Cody died in the shower. Apparently, cats do that shit, find some bathroom corner where they just go and die. I was at my grandmother's funeral when he died and flew into Baltimore on the way home. When I walked in, Dana said they'd already gotten rid of the box with Cody's body. It was weird being in the shower after that. I mean, it was already unclean to begin with but then we had the essence of cat death upon us as we jammed into that little half-room. I cried and cried and thought about the yellow rose Dana had sent me when my grandmother died. There were no roses for Cody.

While we were together, Dana had a good friend named Pluto. Pluto was sexy and into yoga and gardening, like Dana. I felt that I had some claim over Pluto because we'd matched on a dating app months before, but we never met up. Pluto came over to Dana's to give her massages, and I would show up a couple days later and cry about the marks on her neck. Once, Pluto practiced cupping on Dana, the energy release technique leaving massive circular marks on her back that caused her a lot of pain and made her not want to have sex. I was devastated. Not only did Dana have some celestially-named masseuse's hickeys all over her, but I couldn't fall asleep cupping her breasts because Pluto beat me to cupping her back.

Dana and I never said we were monogamous, but we had this pretty shitty dynamic where we would quietly compete with one another to see who could fuck more people in our respective cities. Instead of suggesting that we close our relationship, I fucked people in club bathrooms while Dana fucked Pluto. We had a lot of fights. I called her babysweet. When we made up, she would ask me to call her that. It still comes up on autocorrect on my phone.

I decided to bring Dana home to Ohio for a punk festival. I got us tickets for Valentine's Day. In truth, I wanted Dana to meet my parents, to prove to them that I had a serious girlfriend, that I had moved on from Veil.

But Dana was really bad at meeting my family. She was perpetually awkward, a triple Leo who could be disagreeable at times. When Dana met my mom, my maternal grandmother had recently had a debilitating stroke. My mom was desperate to see a light at the end of the tunnel for her rapidly declining mother. She became attached to this story of a family who took in a wounded baby magpie. It was a true story, of an active young mother who became paralyzed in a fall, how she felt no desire to keep going until this little baby bird arrived on her doorstep, needing help. It's actually a beautiful story, the photographer dad documenting the family raising this magpie, the bird sleeping on the kids' pillows, riding on the mother's wheelchair. Eventually, the magpie grew up and got better and flew away, but still came back to the family's house sometimes as if to check in on them.

My mom told Dana and me the story with tears in her eyes. It was breaking my heart, watching her watch her mother die slowly. When Dana and I packed up and drove two hours south to the punk festival, she was quiet. I asked her what she was thinking, and she asked me if my mom really believed in that magpie shit.

When we got to the festival, Dana puked in the bathroom from drinking, and I stood alone in the crowd, a familiar gait catching my eye. I wasn't wearing my glasses, but I knew immediately: it was Veil. It was Veil with their arms crossed, back to me, standing next to their best friend, on whose floor we had made passionate love the last time I was in this city. I wanted so badly to approach them, to look into their brown eyes and see if I could still see my friends , to say *fuck you* or *I love you* or *please take me back, oh love of my life.* I didn't do any of these things because Dana came back from the bathroom. I told Dana to kiss me in case Veil looked over, and she told me that it felt like shit to be used to make my ex jealous. We fought the whole way home. We fought so much I got out of the car and kicked a concrete wall. We pulled over to fight, we pulled over to fuck. It's just how we were.

A couple weeks later, Rita and I got kicked out of our housing. We were living in a shitty basement room with black mold and asbestos. We'd really cleaned the place up, including the entire trash-filled backyard onto which our room opened out. We hung fairy lights and mirrors and punk posters, and Rita did the dishes for everyone in the house. One day the housemates just sent us a text that one of us had to move out. Rita and I were a package deal, so there was no question that we were both leaving. Crying while we moved our stuff out in the middle of the night, so as not to interact with any housemates, Rita went back in and pissed on the carpet.

We stashed our stuff at my art gallery manager's house, and my dad put us up in a hotel for a couple nights until we could figure something out. I was a mess.

Dana and I had fought that week, and I was posting petty shit about her on Instagram like the mature person I am. When Rita and I got to the hotel, I had a voicemail from Dana. When I pressed play, I realized that it was clearly an accident, that Dana didn't know she had called me. And she was talking shit, about me, to her roommates. I decided at this time that I would jump out of the hotel window, but it was hard to open, and Rita was supposed to be back from work soon. So, I stayed, one eye on the windowpane, promising myself to make it to therapy the following day.

When I wound up in the hospital about twenty-four hours later, I texted Dana desperately from the ER. I told her my therapist put me in an Uber and sent me to the closest psych ward, that my stuff was being taken away and that I loved her despite the voicemail. I remember distinctly that she said, "You are loved," rather than, "I love you." And then they took my phone away.

I had a lot of time to think about Dana during that long night in the psych ward. The showers were freezing, and I was like, *What the fuck is this? One Flew Over the Cuckoo's Nest?* I mean, Jesus. A shower fit for a dead cat. I wrote about her on the slip of paper I found in the common room, in pencil because pens weren't allowed, since you can do some serious harm with a pen nib. We didn't have shoelaces either. When my dad and Rita sweet talked the night shift nurse into letting me out early the next day, I told Dana I was going back to Ohio to recover. She told me she had painted her walls.

A shit poem I gave to Dana after admitting that I loved her

Mistake Poem

1.

your chapped whiskey mouth

my eyes unfocused, waiting

"I think I love you."

Thick red basket swing

carries our bodies, hovers.

Did you just thank me?

that song fills my head—

The one about playground love—

Can't see anymore.

2.

think I've fallen down

Oh wait—you're still here with me

Say something, I plead.

Your friends talking loud

My lonesome overheating

Absorb your triumph

I'd wanted to say

"I loved you at the harbor"

The sandwiches day.

3.

How the first time love

Poured from my skin onto yours

Was months ago now—

The pilot venture

your roommates on the velvet couch

Me scratching your arm

Your eyes a big screen

My fingers, three times, touched you

"I" and "love" and "you"

4.

We traverse bridges

Lit up, lagging behind friends

Will you say it now?

I kiss you frankly

As we cross pavement threshold

Your quiet burns so.

Written down, you say,

Is the date you will love me.

Can I wait that long?

Subject Name _____   **Date**_____

Since your hospitalization, how often have you been bothered by any of the following problems? Circle your response.

	Not at all	Some	Often	Nearly all of the time
Little interest or pleasure in doing things	0	1	2	3
Feeling down, depressed, or hopeless	0	1	2	3
Trouble falling or staying asleep, or sleeping to much	0	1	2	3
Feeling tired or having little energy	0	1	2	3
Poor appetite or overeating	0	1	2	3
Feeling bad about yourself – or that you are a failure or have let your family down	0	1	2	3
Trouble concentrating on things, such as reading the newspaper or watching television	0	1	2	3
Moving or speaking so slowly that other people could have noticed. Or the opposite – being so fidgety or restless that you have been moving around a lot more than usual	0	1	2	3
Thoughts that you would be better off dead, or of hurting yourself	0	1	2	3

Total: _____

*Adapted from the original PHQ-9 developed by Drs. Robert L. Spitzer, Janet B.W. Williams, Kurt Kroenke and colleagues.

VIII. Must've Done Something Right

Shortly after I got out of the hospital, I decided it was time to try having sex again. Dana had been weird about some of the people I'd wanted to sleep with, telling me I couldn't fuck a couple because that was self-objectification, telling me I had a *type* when I wanted to get railed by a butch strap on. But Dana wasn't there, so I did fuck the couple, the boy who was the pancake server at my favorite diner, and the girl who I was just fucking pancake boy to get to. When we took a break during the threesome, he went to make us Trader Joe's samosas in the microwave and his girlfriend sat on my face. He said, "I see you two got started," with a pang of something like sadness when he walked back in with the plate of food.

I started going on a lot of dates, having more casual sex than before. The butch strap on thing happened a lot, and I didn't say *but I'm a top* because I just wanted to get fucked so hard I couldn't think. A cute masc named Mel was my lover for a time, and they were fixated with turning me into a bottom. They would get behind me, doggie-style, and fuck me with the strap-on, which actually didn't feel like anything, although I pretended to moan. I gave them shit about not wanting to have public sex and they got mad, so I went to a drag show to find someone else to hook up with.

That's where I found Dove.

Dove was performing under a stage name, a play on their being from Florida, because Floridians are weirdos. Dove was a fairly well-known local drag king; they wore a glitter beard and bound their chest and packed their boxers with a pair of socks. That night on stage, they were stripping to some emo song, and I sat in the front row. They were pretty into audience participation, so they frequently leapt off-stage to serenade awestruck queers hoping for a chance with them. My friend who is not my friend anymore sat next to me and said, "Damn. He is hot." I nodded my agreement but didn't say anything, and then out of nowhere, he was singing to me with his hand on my knee. He did this again later in the performance. What I didn't know was that his Tinder date was there, watching him serenade me. Afterwards, as my not-friend and I left to go for milkshakes next door, I saw Dove in their glitter beard drinking alone.

A couple nights later, I decided to shoot my shot. I looked up Dove's drag page on Instagram and quickly typed out a message and hit send before I could chicken out:

"Hey you touched my leg twice last night while you were performing LMK if you'd like to fuck sometime."

A few hours of nervous anticipation later, I had a DM back: "I'm interested."

On our first date, I was so nervous I got ridiculously high before meeting them at a local dive bar. I walked down the big hill in DC's Bloomingdale neighborhood and saw them standing at the bottom. I ripped my vape and walked right up and kissed them.

"*Hello!*" they said, smiling. I told Dove I didn't drink, so we abandoned the bar in favor of fried green tomatoes across the street. I wanted to know everything about them. I looked at their chest through their open button-down with UFOs on it.

"How old are you?" was my first question.

"Guess."

"Um, twenty-seven?" I was twenty-four at the time.

"Next month, I will be ten years older than you."

"What!"

Dove explained the transmasculine phenomenon of looking much younger than you really are. I knew this already. Remember Leo, from the sex party? He was in his fifties, and I was in my early twenties. Dove did look like a little boy with their outer space shirt and wide eyes. I invited them to get on the back of one of those rent-a-scooters, and soon we were doing donuts in the parking lot where my queer soccer team met. It was dark and the only lights were on the field, where we played all our games. I asked what they were doing for the rest of their life as we sat on the curb. They told me they wanted to lie down with me. We army crawled under the chain link fence to get onto the soccer field and we fucked for the first time then and there, under those bright lights. They were a bottom. A match made in heaven.

We were inseparable after that. Our first date lasted almost 48 hours. After our night on the soccer field, they slept over in my basement room I shared with Rita, getting tangled in my glittery curtains above the bed. The following morning, we went to breakfast at the popular Bloomingdale café, and then I accompanied them to work. They were a dogwalker and I went on every single dog walk they had booked that day. The first picture Dove ever took of me is from that afternoon: I'm holding a scruffy little Pomeranian, smiling abundantly in all black and wearing their baseball hat. When we were finished with the dogs, we fucked in their oceanic turquoise room, so hard that I fell off the bed upside down.

Our love story was forged by a shared affinity for ironic Christian rock. Dove had converted to evangelicalism when they were a preteen, and ended up converting their parents, too. Picture all the blowup pool baptism shit and you'll get the picture. I remember the time Dove showed me the video reenactment of the Passion of Christ from the summer camp where they were a counselor. It was on YouTube for all to see. I said it was horrific. They said I was the first person to take their trauma seriously. Relient K was our mutual band of choice. Everything about it was appealing: its misspelled title, its evangelical roots, my nostalgia for being made to listen to it in middle school by my best friend. Now that was true emo. They have this song called "Must've Done

Something Right," which kinda became our song. On a beach trip right before I moved to Spain, Dove posted a photo of us on Instagram; I'm snuggled in their lap, they're smiling down at me with lyrics by Relient K as the caption: "If anyone can make me a better person you could/All I gotta say is I must've done something good."

Dove and I met about three months before my move to Spain. Disillusioned with my pre-Dove life in DC, I had been accepted to one of those mostly bullshit teaching programs at a public school in Madrid, supposedly helping Spanish kids learn English. I was fresh out of the psych ward and needed a change and later I wondered whether Dove or Spain were it. We had one beautiful, perfect summer together, to which they would forever refer to as "our summer." After that, I left.

We FaceTimed every day while I was abroad. Our nighttime routine became Dove singing to me on the guitar through my screen until I fell asleep. My favorite was when they sang "Hey There Delilah" because their voice broke a little on the part that goes, "...A thousand miles is pretty far, but they've got planes and trains and cars, I'd walk to you if I had no other way..."

Dove punctuated my year in Madrid with visits. Together we adventured from the Costa Blanca coastline to rowboats in Sevilla. We loved desperately, but the little bristles between our decade apart itched at my skin. I wondered why they didn't have friends their own age. I wondered why they wanted to date a twenty-four-year-old. I wondered how long I could put off settling down with them. And the facets of our nonmonogamy brought a lot of tension: we'd never officially agreed on monogamy at any point, but we'd been functionally exclusive during "our summer" because we were too infatuated and codependent to see anyone else. At one point, a lover whom I'd met in Scotland came to visit me. I essentially ignored them and dumped them on Rita for two weeks while I slept at Dove's.

Dove had a woman they called their "Once A Month" whom they slept with approximately...you guessed it. One time, I met the Once A Month. She had big blue eyes, like me, but dark, long hair. We were at our favorite music venue in DC, at a regular dance party. I think it was 80s themed. I always went to the 80s themed nights. I liked going with Dove because they were actually alive in the 80s. On this occasion, Dove ran into some friends getting drinks at the bar, including the Once A Month. I was wearing a lacy baby blue bodysuit with roses over the nipples, and I was covered in hickeys from Dove. Excited to show me off to their friends and former lover, Dove pulled down my top to reveal the darkest mark on my chest, nearly exposing my tits, right there in the bar. I went out to get some air after that, feeling violated. Dove chased after me while stopping to puke up their beer in a trash can. When Rita came to pick me up, she immediately asked Dove what I'd done this time.

I told myself moving to Spain was the right thing for me, traumatized by the mental hospital and escaping a bad housing situation, but Dove couldn't wait for me to get back. It is a point of pride now for me that I didn't return solely to be with them, though I never expected to lose them only when we were both back on the same side of the ocean. I think, mostly, Dove couldn't wait for me to stop fucking other people. I'd call them the day after sleeping with someone else, often waking them up first thing. Sometimes when I called, they were already awake, making eggs or doing yoga.

"What are you doing awake, baby?" I'd say.

"Having a morning, baby," they'd say with a soft smile.

Once, they called me, crying, while I was in an Uber with a girl I was about to fuck for the first time. I mouthed *lo siento* to the girl while she took her shoes off and I sat in her living room, comforting Dove. "Baby, I'm with someone else right now...can I call you tomorrow?" When I put the phone down, I rushed to the bed to join a girl whose name I barely knew.

Dove gave me a ring. A beautiful, green cut stone. It fit me perfectly in all the ways. Green is my favorite color for a rock. In return, I gave Dove a lot of heartache. The summer after "our summer," a few months before I left Spain, I met Mar, who would become my lover. I spent a lot of time lying to Dove about how much time I was spending with Mar. My plan for the end of the summer was to move back to the States, to catch the end of the season with Dove and to recreate the magic of that first summer together. Only now there was Mar, and I didn't want to leave.

Dove asked me to move in with them in DC, but I said no and moved to Boston. I invited Dove to visit me for a lovely week spent in the mountains of New Hampshire right after I arrived back, and then I broke up with them over the phone as soon as they stepped in the door from driving home.

After meeting Mar, I questioned my decision to leave Spain after one year. Staying for a year had been the plan all along, especially because Dove and I had gotten together immediately before I left. *It's only a year, baby,* I'd promise. Truthfully, I had no plan but knew I needed to get out of DC, far away from college and the hospital and a handful of exes. And after my initial bout of mental health treatment, I came to love Spain. That said, after being stuck in my *piso* for two months of Spanish lockdown, I was ready to return to the States to see my loved ones and get a dose of as much normalcy as we could collectively muster.

I met Dove on the precipice of the unknown, and I met Mar on the brink of returning to the known. I fell in love both ways. And both ways hurt.

IX. Besitos

The first time I saw you, you wore a Halloween mask that your sister gave you. Not like a scary one from a party store, but a cloth one that covered half your face when we thought that kept us safe. You told me you loved Halloween like the Scorpio you are. I led you to my favorite Madrid cafe, swearing by the honeyed matcha. You quickly realized how poor my Spanish is, and we switched to English to save me the embarrassment. It was still the afternoon when we went back to my place in Lavapiés, climbed all those stairs to sit on my bed while I realized I actually had no game anymore. You sat politely and then leaned in, asking your question: "Do you want to keeeees?"

The first time we had sex, then and there, I blew your mind. Not to brag. When I fuck you, your eyes always do this thing where they go a little unfocused for a while and you take deep breaths and yell *no pares.* I hadn't felt electricity like that since Veil. I didn't know I could feel it anymore. I was embarrassed by my pronunciation of your name. I couldn't quite get the accent right. Turns out my shitty Spanish didn't matter in bed. Turns out you don't need names in bed.

In Spain, everyone has what they refer to as their *pueblo,* which basically means ancestral village in this case. Where they're *really* from. Where their people are. You invited me to yours on what felt like a whim, and I obliged you, taking the train from Madrid to Avila where I got stuck inside the train car and mouthed words at you until someone got me out. Your twin sister was there. She looks nothing like you, except for the smile. It was at the pueblo that you told me your birth name, kissed me under that great spherical rock that looms over the village. We fell in love at the pueblo. I made you my butch, I made you my bitch. You called me *"mi reina."*

The truth is, I'm not sure yet if you're different, even if I have promised myself to you a thousand times. I don't even know how to write about you, *mi alma gemela.* I lost Dove because of you, and it was worth it. I lost the fantasy of a future together. I left my job so I could travel to be with you. I lost my heart to the point where I don't even want to be gay anymore because queer love, true love, our love, has devastated me. I abandoned myself for you and you found someone else. You did to me what I did to Dove.

I want to delete our entire two-year Whatsapp thread, lose all those I Love Yous. But I won't.

100 I Love Yous

1. Do you remember the time you met me in the dark?

2. Fue todo.

3. I fear I'm getting better.

4. And if I live, I will have to go to a movie theater. That's alright because I love movie theaters, but here in my sickbed I can't imagine a big screen lighting up the darkness, just the small one of my phone, where I watch to see if the word "online" appears under your name. I don't know that I can handle such large-scale luminosity, even in that pitch-black, popcorn-stinking escape room.

5. I hope I live long enough to marry you.

6. Is that manipulative to say?

7. When I see the green dot of your avatar, my heart drops because who could you be looking at but me?

8. The scars on my wrist look red today, like my lips. Yours are more pink, like the sky in its polluted sunset beauty.

9. I never liked sunsets unless they were pink.

10. Is *embalse* masculine or feminine?

11. It's the two-year anniversary of meeting the love of my life and I am selling masturbation videos to a middle-aged man on Instagram with his kid in his profile pic.

12. Jumping into commitment from afar makes it harder to overcome things.

13. You tell me to use my talent first and then fuck an old guy if that doesn't get me a publishing deal. I say fucking people is my talent.

14. Don't spend too much money on the ring.

15. I thought I heard you call my name...

16. Which one?

17. All of them.

18. I cannot handle the reciprocal aspect of nonmonogamy.

19. I have a new therapist and I will work with her on the self-harm thing, okay?

20. Please don't do with her what we did in that special place.

21. I wish your grandparents had met my grandparents.

22. On the train to London, I ask you if you eat fish, and you say, "only you, baby."

23. I tell you that's a misogynist joke and

24. You are sorry.

25. The best part of fucking you is feeling my mouth twist into shapes of letters and discovering I do not know your name.

26. But I do: remember that awful taxi ride in Scotland where I rebooked your flight from the

backseat? I had to tell them your old name, the one your mother gave you.

27. I thought: this is love.

28. I can taste the sunlight on your skin.

29. I can taste the sunlight on your skin.

30. I can taste the sunlight on your skin–

31. I feel so guilty for that thing I said two years ago, the one I never told you about.

32. I've said a lot of things in desperation.

33. My psychiatrist tells me the kids used to overdose on cough syrup, and I smile because he shouldn't be telling me that. That's why I can't take Lithium, after all, I have a tendency to want

a little too much of a good thing.

34. Everything in moderation.

35. When I was a child, my father once told me that if someone out there really wants you dead, they'll find a way to kill you.

36. Recently I've asked, does that apply to yourself?

37. I look up suicide statistics of unrequited lovers.

38. The internet advises me that they are low these days.

39. You pinch the barbell through my nipple with your teeth in the ramparts. Its shape like an arrow threatens to pierce the soft skin of my breast, whose days may be numbered. Double mastectomy Saint Sebastian chuckles in bed with us as blood pools in my belly button.

40. In the cave's cool mouth I squat like the porn star they wanted, begging me to piss.

41. Hero of my dreams/ why do you look like a girl?/ I ask to the night.

42. I know the answer/ says the darkness to my mind/ you always loved wounds.

43. The wind tousles my hair like a lover.

44. You are the lover.

45. The best thing, besides you, is to touch the sea.

46. I wrote a book of my love for you tonight.

47. Why is it that you always ask me to read to you?

48. Someone once told me I have a sexy voice, and I wonder how it will change and if you will like the changes.

49. Haiku for our living bodies in a cemetery: shadow of the grave/ love you more than anything/ kiss me on the dead.

50. I nibble your palm like a summer peach, and you tell me I make your underwear juicy.

51. You say over breakfast, "Did you ask me to marry you last night?"

52. I look down at the porridge you made us because I don't use the stove and say,

53. "Maybe."

54. We are not talking as I am writing this.

55. What about the first time you held my hand?

56. Do you remember that, the first time you held my hand?

57. We walked up the hill to Lavapiés one hot night, and I freaked out and told you that this felt more intimate than sex.

58. "Baby," you say when you wake up, "which stop is ours?"

59. I love you more than anything.

60. I know that isn't healthy.

61. There is a portrait of your grandparents in their little village house, and I see your face in your grandfather's, not smiling.

62. You laugh when I tell you I want you to get me pregnant.

63. I still listen to that playlist I made you two years ago.

64. You don't know this, but I listened to it so much that I forgot to listen to the one my partner made me.

65. You don't know this either, but that long playlist of love songs by my partner was their last-ditch effort to reconnect, and I pretended I listened to it, but it was a lie because instead of listening to it in my room like I said I was, I was making love to you.

66. Months later, my partner and I were driving in the mountains of New Hampshire when I complimented their song choices.

67. "Do you know what this is from?" they asked, choking a little on their words. I had a feeling but waited for them to tell me anyway.

68. "It's the playlist I made for you when you were in Spain. You told me you listened. When you were with them."

69. Do you remember the time you fucked me on the rocks in the middle of a shallow woodland river? There were kids nearby.

70. Do you remember that on the way back to the bus stop, we saw a man who had fallen down a ditch with his head bleeding and the police standing over him?

71. I often wonder if he is dead.

72. While you are fucking the girl you've known since childhood, I am editing your older brother's master's thesis.

73. I tell you he's a good writer.

74. Do you know I keep that swimsuit that makes me feel weird about my gender because you kissed me while I was wearing it?

75. Of course you don't; I haven't told you.

76. When I make you sad while we're on the phone, I wait for my dog to bark because when you say his name there is lightness in your voice again.

77. I once laid beside you in your parents' bed and held you while you cried about your ex-girlfriend. I repeated something I'd seen online: I told you that you hadn't met everyone who was going to love you yet and

78. I was right.

79. Every time I see a picture of the lovers' lock bridge over the Seine, I zoom in to see if one of them is ours. I can never tell but I know it's there.

80. Exactly three times, you have asked me to get matching tattoos,

and I laugh nervously because the one that I want is a black band around my finger.

81. You tell me you're not into skinny femmes and it makes my night.

82. I've been saying buenos sueños for years now, and you only just told me it's wrong.

83. You're kind that way.

84. I'm worried if I live long enough, you will leave me.

85. Please don't leave me.

86. I wonder if I have Borderline Personality Disorder.

87. I wonder if I'd tell you if I did.

88. What I don't say to you on the phone is get out now.

89. We could build a beautiful life together, and I could take it away at any moment; at any moment I could die.

90. I suppose we could all die at any moment, and

91. that's what makes my love for you so precious.

92. When I ask you to marry me in your half-asleep state, we are on my aunt's pull-out couch. You smile with your eyes closed and say, "but you mean nonmonogamously, right?"

93. I say yes baby and pretend you're not breaking my heart.

94. Te quiero.

95. Y yo a ti.

96. I bought you a ring with three moons on it because I would love you in any sky.

97. I'm sorry.

98. I have emptied my heart.

99. Do you remember the time you met me in the dark?

-
-
-
-
-
-
-
-
-
-
-
-
-
-
-
-
-
-
-
-

100. Fue todo.

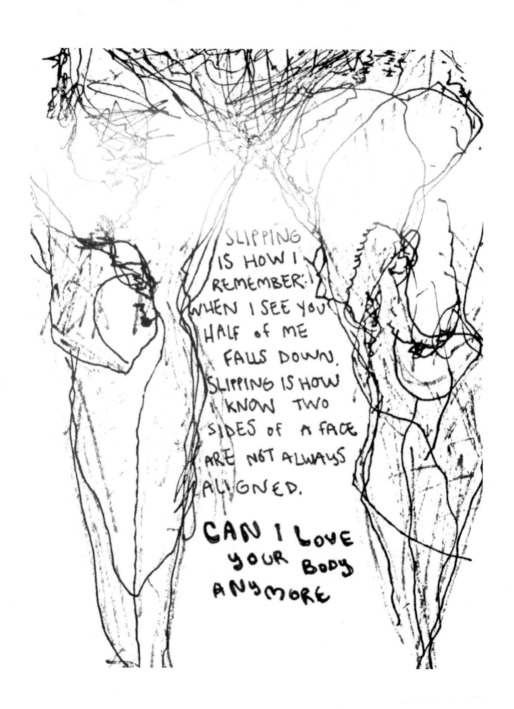

SLIPPING
IS HOW I
REMEMBER:
WHEN I SEE YOU
HALF OF ME
FALLS DOWN.
SLIPPING IS HOW
I KNOW TWO
SIDES OF A FACE
ARE NOT ALWAYS
ALIGNED.

CAN I LOVE
YOUR BODY
ANYMORE

78

Two Totally Shit Tattoos

What the fuck am I looking at? You might be wondering.
Well, it's a scan of my upper left thigh, complete with its oldest
adornment: a pair of stick-n-poked scissors by Mort. I'm aware that

it looks really bad. You can't tell in the scan, but the ink is all blown out. Internal bleeding-like. I ironically wanted it because, you know, scissoring, but I had my boyfriend do it because he was the artist. This is after I'd come out as queer, but lesbianism was still just my academic interest. We were in my tiny dorm room in northern England, using India ink and a sewing needle. It hurt like hell. In return, I gave him a shitty bug, kind of caterpillar-esque. He used to call me Buggie. I have absolutely no idea why.

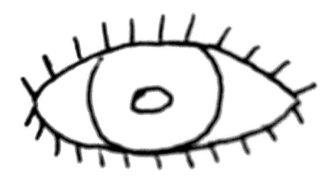

This second one is a drawing by me of a tattoo I have on the right side of my ribcage, done by Veil. I can't capture it myself on camera, so I decided to draw it. It's Veil's trademark eye, a kind of tag when they did graffiti and often their signature on paintings. It was surprisingly emotional drawing this myself. I don't think I'd ever tried to replicate one of Veil's eyes, or at least, I haven't in years. It's the only thing I have left of Veil's art. Unlike most of the drawings in this book, this one is new. I did it today. I couldn't get the eyelashes right: on my body, they are more plentiful, but straight like little arrows, in Veil's confident hand. In return, I tattooed their birth name under their left breast. I just found a picture of it on my camera roll. Now that they've had top surgery, I wonder if it's still there.

A Note for Mort

All these years later, I visited Harvey Pekar's grave. It was chock full of tchotchkes, pencils so weathered their erasers were black, little comic figurines. I left a flower there for you and me.

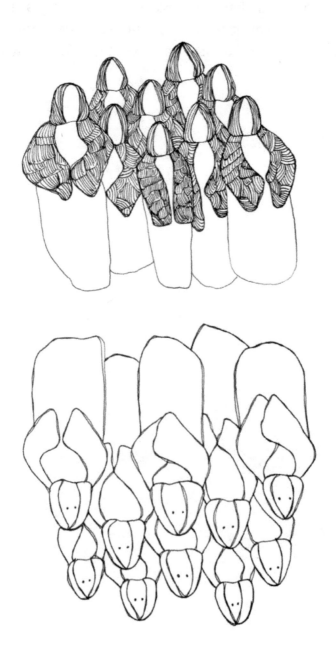

X. LOOKING FOR AUGUSTINE

I always thought it was kind of kinky that Sex and Love Addicts Anonymous has the super covert codename of "The Augustine Fellowship." When I was in undergrad studying art history, we learned about the Confessions of Augustine, the saint's recounting of his sexual exploits before relegating himself to celibacy forevermore. Even then, as a horny college student, this shit totally stumped me. I remember going back to my dorm room and asking my roommates whether they ever jacked off to the academic material they learned in their seminars. The roommates, who studied International Affairs and Math respectively, gasped, "No!"

Art history is pretty much the sluttiest subject. Perusing medieval Books of Hours with tits everywhere, decoding the ornate and highly sexualized reliefs on temples throughout the world, studying the nudes of genre painting. At the time, I was still dating Veil, who would come down to DC for weeks at a time to stay in my tiny dorm bed with me. They worked at a vegan bakery and woke up early to make niche cupcake flavors, and then took a ton of time off all at once to come fuck me because the bakery was owned by a friend. When Veil visited, a weird sort of academic explosion happened for me. On one hand, I was skipping class, a lot, to fuck, and on the other hand, one of Veil's most endearing qualities was that they were an avid learner. And they thought I was just about the smartest person they had ever met. So in between orgasms, I read to them from my art history notes and textbooks. Sometimes I wrote essays while they went down on me. School felt like fodder for sex.

The introduction to Augustine's *Confessions* reads:

"[That]...the author is writing of a somewhat distant past, as we shall have occasion to point out more fully afterwards, must be taken into account when reading the *Confessions.* Augustine wrote at the request of friends who begged him to commit to writing these recollections of his former life to which he often referred in private conversation. He consented for the characteristic reason that he desired his friends to mourn and rejoice along with him as they followed his retrospect of past years, and on his behalf to give thanks to God."

I mean, FUCK me! Isn't this exactly what I'm doing? Putting down my adolescent exploits to stain the page? To show the people around me how I've grown? To process the somewhat distant past? It's interesting to me that the story of my sexuality, blooming at the age of fifteen, covers almost exactly the same amount of time elapsed as Augustine's confessions of his sins. Among other things, Augustine is the patron saint of printers. Meaning writers. Meaning I'm part of a long ass lineage of sex addicted pen-holders who can't get enough of their own literary self-punishment. And I sort of love it.

I decided to quit *The Augustine Fellowship* once I had a poem published about it. It felt wrong to go back after that. The poem goes like this:

Masturbating to the Sex & Love Addicts Anonymous Basic Text on a Wednesday Night

Forgive me, nonexistent higher power, for I have sinned.

Gxd grant me the serenity to cum before I feel guilty, the courage to climax before I experience shame, and the wisdom to not tell anyone about this, ever.

The guy in the book, Rich, keeps telling me about his years of sexual disarray and emotional dissatisfaction. And let me tell you, it is turning me the fuck on.

I'm sorry for being a sex addict. And I'm sorry for writing about it. I am one month into my program and all I can show for it is a dog-eared 12-step guide discarded next to my vibrator.

I promise to go to a meeting first thing in the morning. To confess and to repent. To receive absolution. To admit I had my tongue out and my legs spread while I read the program literature.

I hope someone punishes me. I hope I am slapped across the face over Zoom. My attendance itself is a form of self-flagellation and when I introduce myself I will look into the camera.

Keep coming back, they tell me. Keep cumming back. Lock me in a room with nothing because I will make love to a book.

I admit that I am powerless.

I mean, it's all true. I showed up to every Zoom meeting with the attitude of "So, who all's hot here?" I fantasized about my friend, the fellow poet, the Brooklyn pole dancer, the former child star turned astral chart reader. There were butch carpenters and TikTok stars. Not to mention Ethan, the older redhead. How the fuck was I supposed to get a sponsor if I just wanted to fuck everyone?

The saving grace of my time in SLAA was Ellie. Ellie was a newly out trans woman with whom I spoke on the phone once each day. She was the entirety of my "fellowship" practice, what they call interpersonal recovery relationships and support in 12-Step. Ellie was in med school in the South and talked me through everything from my relationship with Em to the possibilities of me starting hormone therapy. In return, I listened to her recount her successes, like showing up to AA with painted nails or letting her daughters see her in a skirt. To me, Ellie was a revelation. Someone whom I had never met and was unlikely to ever meet, but someone who cared intensely about me and my recovery from a thousand miles away. Some days, Ellie and I cried a little on the phone together, and other days, we lifted each other up in our successes. Ellie championed me, and I stopped returning her calls. I still feel bad about this.

Augustine wrote: "I held my heart back from positively accepting anything, since I was afraid of another fall, and in this condition of suspense I was being all the more killed."

I read my poem about masturbating to the SLAA literature aloud at a performance I gave in a gallery downtown. The piece was called "Pop Up Confessional: An Indirect Study in Forgiveness," during which I performed the poem and then asked everyone in the audience to take a scrap of paper and write down a confession. When they were finished, I collected and then redistributed each confession, so the secrets had a new owner. The finale of the piece was when the new secret keeper read their adopted confession aloud to the group. There was a lot of heavy shit in there.

Childhood abuse, utter loneliness, pent up desires. After the oration, I passed out handwritten stickers that said I AM ABSOLVED. It was honestly more for me than for them.

And with this public performance about being a sex addict to a shit ton of people, in the flesh, who I didn't know, I was free of SLAA. I followed everyone hot on Instagram so I could keep peering at them through my screen, and that was that.

The thing about Augustine is that he was privy to the passion of the world and he gave it up. In SLAA, they would call that being "anorexic," or cutting yourself off from healthy relationships entirely until you become a spinsterish recluse. Okay I added that last part, but you get what I'm trying to say. If I prayed, I would pray to the patron saint of printers. *Why have you forsaken me in this Zoom room and beyond? How am I to find respite without turning into you?* The difference between Augustine and me, two relatively reflective if not disastrously horny people, is what we decided to do with our addictive tendencies.

Augustine repented. I didn't.

He wrote:

Late have I loved you, beauty so old and so new: late have I loved you. And see, you were within and I was in the external world and sought you there, and in my unlovely state I plunged into those lovely created things which you made. You were with me, and I was not with you. The lovely things kept me far from you, though if they did not have their existence in you, they had no existence at all. You called and cried out loud and shattered my deafness. You were radiant and resplendent, you put to flight my blindness. You were fragrant, and I drew in my breath and now pant after you. I tasted you, and I feel but hunger and thirst for you. You touched me, and I am set on fire to attain the peace which is yours.

FOUR BOYS IN AUGUST
(MY MONTH OF BISEXUALITY)

BOY 1
SPOONS ME AS HE TELLS ME TO TAKE DEEP BREATHS. LATER TELLS ME IT MIGHT BE BENEFICIAL FOR ME TO TAKE A BREAK FROM SEX.

BOY 2
COMES OVER AT 3AM. WE GHOST EACH OTHER.

BOY 3
MAYBE ISN'T A BOY AT ALL. DANGLY EARRINGS IS NICE TO ME.

BOY 4
TELLS ME HE'S GOT A BIG LOAD AS HE ROLLS OFF OF ME. BEST PART IS THE BACK RUB. NO CONTACT INFO.

Orgasm Looks Good on You

he says as he kisses my face. I am panting. I am full of happiness. I am the happiest I have been all summer. At the hands of a man, no less.

The night I opened the door for him it was late, the early hours of the morning, really. He stood at the bottom of the porch stairs. As he walked up, I felt my staunch lesbiansism shift a little. *You're shorter than I pictured*, he says. *You're taller than I pictured*, I say.

Now we are in bed in his fancy Cambridge apartment and we won't sleep a wink. As he fucks me from behind, I think I hear him accidentally call me baby. *You shouldn't cum inside me*, I say, *I'm not on any kind of birth control*. He says, *I have a condom on*. I say, *Still*.

I haven't so much as touched a man in three years. I haven't had an orgasm with one in maybe ten. *You taste so good*. I warn him I'm probably no good at giving blowjobs anymore, and he tells me I'm full of shit as he fills my mouth. *Muscle memory, I guess*, I say with a self-conscious smile.

I tell myself it's not really like being with a man because he has a girl's name. Because he's pretty, like a girl. Because he's bisexual.

A week later he texts me that it's gotten complicated, and we shouldn't see each other anymore. I post on my Instagram story, *Let's fuck once and then watch each other's Instagram stories forever until one of us dies*. He sends me the fire react emoji in response and tells me I ought to take a break from sex.

I say he's an asshole.

XI. SUPERFICIAL CUTTING

I'm writing this from just north of the Ozarks, Arkansas. What the hell are you doing in Arkansas, L, you might ask? I'm taking a break from my outpatient treatment for Bipolar Disorder to do a writing residency that I was granted a year ago. Yes, I'm back in outpatient because I'm a failure at recovery. Just kidding, my therapists always get mad when I say that shit, but according to the tenets of Narrative Therapy, it is the "story I have internalized."

But here I am in what was recently referred to me as a flyover state, putting these stories I have internalized down on paper. And you know what? I think I fucking love it here. Sure, my life is a total mess: I left my job, I'm in a full-time recovery program, now I'm in the middle of nowhere, my relationships are a mess as usual. I don't know what's next for me other than returning to outpatient after this brief Southern writing stint.

"Do you hear any voices that other people can't hear?"

"Only the ones coming from the grotto."

My partial hospitalization program has been virtual, so I am back in a Zoom room where I started. Next week, when I return home, it will finally be in person again. Part of me is excited to see who is hot in real life. The other part of me is trying to shut the first part of me off. Most days I have a one-on-one appointment with my personal clinician, who is kind and action-oriented, even if she does speak to me in a way you might speak to a kid. She asks me if I'm having any hallucinations, if I'm hearing things. I dutifully tell her no, no, I'm not, it's just that I want to kill myself all the time. She writes this down with her brow furrowed.

The part of Northwest Arkansas I'm in is called Eureka Springs, a hippie town a little less than fifty miles from Fayetteville. There's no way to get here aside from hiring a driver or taking an Uber, which generally only exist on weekends. When I sat in the car for the hour and a half drive from the airport to the writer's retreat, my mom called me to make sure I wasn't being kidnapped. "Good to check in on these long drives," she said. The driver, who was a lovely person and absolutely did not kidnap me, dropped me off on a curving road in front of a series of Frank Lloyd Wright-inspired houses, built into the hillside. I rolled my suitcase down a set of stone stairs and burst into a quaint little office with cookies on the table and two blonde women to greet me. I only winced a little as they called me "she" and made sure to compliment the decor. My room is so beautiful I thought, "Damn, I can't wait to fuck myself here later."

The town is called Eureka Springs for the natural springs that seem to pop up everywhere. Just across from the luxurious cabin-house that I have all to myself is Grotto Spring, which is at the bottom of another stone staircase intricately adorned with a floral metal handrail and with a drippy, man-made cave mouth. When you get down the stairs to the same level as the spring, the temperature shift literally takes your breath away. Arkansas in August is hot and muggy, but the air in the spring cavern is so cool that you can see your breath. Stepping into the cave's entryway, something glows at the back of the rocky room: a small shrine, with a candle for the Virgin and some trinkets left by passersby. My fellow writer-in-residence tells me there's something different there every time she goes in, whether it's a photograph, tea candles, or a cigarette. I learn that postwar, people traveled for miles to take in the healing waters. When I tell this to my parents, my dad tells me to swim in it.

"How many days in the last week have you felt worthless?"

"All of them, my friend."

When I take an off-record call from a former psychiatrist of mine, I forget I'm in Arkansas and I mess up with the time difference. I can't see this doctor anymore because of getting kicked off my parents' insurance, but he makes time for me anyway.

I can't quite hear him over speaker phone and I imagine the phone wires getting crossed between all the flyover states in between us. He tells me I'm a tough cookie in his nearly undetectable Spanish accent. He asks me how my relationship is, and I say tumultuous. He says I make an ideal patient.

The thing with virtual outpatient, just like virtual Sex and Love Addicts Anonymous, is that people ARE hot, even through a screen. I find myself falling in love with the therapist, who looks just like Mar: I've never been able to resist big brown eyes. On my last day before heading to the writing residency, this therapist thanks me for my bravery and tells me I've been a pleasure to have in group. I tell them, "I love you, bro, I'll see you when I get back." The other therapist I have swiped on, on every dating app, but we never match because I think if they swiped on me it would be illegal. Maybe not illegal, but heavily unethical, I'm guessing. I make an Instagram poll of whether I should fuck one of the outpatient therapists and everyone says no. Well, almost everyone.

"I'm sorry to hear you've been having health issues..." starts off every email I've received this summer. I'm sorry too. The off-record psychiatrist tells me to try an experimental psychedelic treatment and I smile because I knew magic mushrooms were good for me. I'm what they call "treatment-resistant." It's really a lot of fun. Jokes aside, I think this is what they call people who are on a shit ton of psychiatric meds already and just don't get better. My cocktail of serotonin doesn't seem to be doing me much good: I feel as though I'm back where I started, having lots of random sex just to feel something, trying to scale back on my self-harm actions. My current doctor calls the rivulets of blood on the outside of my wrist, "superficial cutting." This makes me laugh every time. *Who are you to say it's superficial?* The intention runs pretty deep.

In outpatient, they make me answer the where and how questions of self-harm and ask whether I have any open wounds. "They're not bad," I say, "I think they're fine." The clinicians nod and write down what I say. Every day at the beginning of group, we have to answer our "MSC": our individual scales of 1-10 indicating Mood, Safety, and Commitment. If your Safety score is below four, the clinician running the group has to tell on you to your individual provider. My Safety is never above a four, so at the end of group each day I get a personalized email asking how likely I am to kill myself that night. I don't want to freak them out or get sent to inpatient again, so I always say that I'm too tired to do anything, and they seem to either buy that or just want to go home for the day.

When I cut, I use a boxcutter. I like this because it feels kind of butch. Cutting with a disposable razor feels too flimsy, especially when it's pink. I like the workman yellow brightness of the boxcutter's little handle and the metallic sheen of the blade, the way you can pop it out bit by bit in a way that reminds me of a slow-moving erection. I am always responsible about cutting. When I enter the bathroom with the boxcutter, I try to make sure no one is home, that my dog is soundly asleep, that I'm not expecting any texts or calls. I grab a paper towel from the kitchen and isopropyl alcohol from under the sink. I clean my arm first and then the blade, rubbing the alcohol-soaked paper over my skin the way they do at the doctor's office. It feels sterile, professional, satisfying. When I bring the blade to the skin, I take a deep breath and smile. At outpatient they tell you smiling a little can help. I want to tell them that bleeding a little can help.

"The first step toward change is identifying the problem behavior."

"What if I don't think of it as a problem?"

In Arkansas, rock juts out everywhere. From between buildings, stairways, healing springs. The rock is a constant presence, which as an Earth sign, I don't mind. It feels like walking along a perennial cliff face, which is pretty on brand with how I feel.

Walking back from town, my residency mate and I notice a haphazard parking spot at the very edge of the land, before the hillside drops off into jagged rock and woods. She comments on how scary this is, how your car could just go right over. I smile and nod. The way the rock looks from above is so beautiful, so cleanly ridged it looks almost laser-cut. In fact, it kind of looks like if God did some superficial cutting too.

Portrait of Me, In Arkansas

I am wandering along a highway with no guardrails, on foot. I am stumbling as I read *The Confessions of St. Augustine,* walking up the hilly street. I am sitting in the karaoke-themed cafe on a light green leather couch, wondering what the fuck I am doing. I am flirting with the older writer, who is the only other person at the residency. I am drinking mocktails with her at a bar we entered because I saw a lesbian sitting at the counter. I am catching her eye as she tells me the pleasure is in the wanting and holds my hands as I tell her I don't want to be alive. I am watching the kids jump off the brick platform to nowhere into the weedy lake. I am thinking of fucking someone's husband. I am wondering how to get high in the middle of nowhere. I am listening to a man at the cafe ask his girlfriend, *Who came on you? It sure as hell wasn't me.* I am riding in the backseat of the gay Uber driver's Jeep, telling him I am also gay and that I would love to meet his four collies. I am double-checking the locks on the door when I find a table, place set for one, even though I am the only one on the premises and I sure as hell didn't set it. I am taking in the ghosts. I am talking to the ghosts. I am fucking myself on the floor with the blinds open so I can see the trees. I am ghosting boys on dating apps. I am ghosting girls on dating apps. I am walking along another highway. I am having dreams that I am pregnant. I am waking up in a cold sweat. I am swimming in the pool of the haunted hotel that looms from the hillside over the town. I am wondering if I should try to write a poem. I am throwing up from anxiety in the cabin bathroom. I am watching the disco lights roll over my hands in the karaoke cafe. I am congratulating myself for going a whole week without fucking a stranger. I am deciding I am just gay after all. I am letting out a deep sigh of relief when I finally get my period. I am wandering along a highway. I am trying not to get bitten by snakes. I am watching the mist roll over the Ozarks. I am dancing in a cave. I am by myself. I am by myself. I am safe here.

Redemption Arc

The truth of this story is that I'm not sure whether there is any redemption arc. From the outside, it might be easier to say *they're right back where they started.* Vaguely bisexual, mentally ill, in full-time treatment for wanting to die. Can you recover from wanting to die? Is a death wish treatable? Is sex addiction real? Can we quantify desire for human intimacy as a disorder? What's the point of pathologizing love?

Hell, I don't know.

What I do know is that my life has a cadence to it, my patterns have patterns. Maybe it all started when I was fifteen, with Mort, but I suspect it started earlier than that, during those long days of childhood listening to the voice inside my head scream.

In group therapy at the hospital, they say *Mental illness is an explanation, not an excuse.* I don't butt heads as much with what they tell me in the hospital anymore because I am surrounded by my peers: people who are just trying to get better, whatever *better* means to them. My years as a sex addict function as an excuse. My time in 12-step was a bandaid. This isn't the case for everyone, but it is for me.

Maybe I'm being harsh with myself, but when the therapists asked me what I wanted to work on, I said, *Extending forgiveness.* Reflecting on my inflexible boundaries. Confronting those boundaries I pretend don't exist in relationships. And I'm starting to see that forgiveness applies to me, too.

So, what do I have to show for fucking half the planet?

Self-awareness. Insight into my self-sabotage. Accountability for destruction.

And maybe, for now, that's enough of a recovery for me.

XII. STILL HERE

Dear _____,

The worst part is that I dream about you almost every night. I don't even know who "you" are anymore. I see your many, contorted faces when I close my eyes, and I wake up happy because in dreams you forgive me.

I'm not sure how to sign off. You know who it's from.

Leighah

I stopped keeping track of the number of people I've fucked when it got to be over fifty. I started fucking boys again as an act of self-harm to break up the cutting. I feel bile rise in my throat when they say things like *You have nice titties* or *I wish more girls were into this sort of thing.* I have a few days left before I am in an outpatient recovery program round three. But there is another shirt that sits in my drawer, under *I'm So Miserable Without You It's Almost Like Having You Here.*

And this one says, *STILL HERE.*

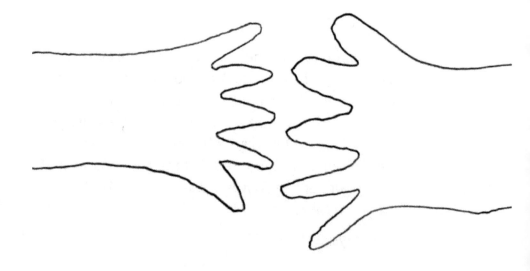

Acknowledgements

The section entitled "100 I Love Yous" was published by Ethel Zine and Micro Press as a chapbook in February 2023. A selection from "100 I Love Yous" was also published in Pom Pom Press, 2022.

The poem "Masturbating to the Sex & Love Addicts Anonymous Basic Text on a Wednesday Night" was published in Anti-Heroin Chic in October 2021.

The prologue of this book was published in Hobart as an essay in February 2023.

The final chapter of this book is named after the work of the artist Ariel Baldwin.

Endless thanks to the many people and places who went into the genesis of this book. This manuscript was completed as the thesis component of the Lesley University MFA in Creative Writing Program under the loving tutelage of Nonfiction faculty Pamela Petro and Kyoko Mori. Thank you to the community of mentors and peers who read the many inceptions of this work with generosity and care. The heart of this book was born at the Writers' Colony at Dairy Hollow in Eureka Springs, Arkansas. Thank you to WCDH for the happiest of solitudes and for your delicious meals. The manuscript's final chapters were written in a cozy barn loft outside of Chalais, France. Thank you to the community of lovers and artists at La Barre for being with me on the last page, particularly to Philippa Gell and Christopher Jewitt for your serendipitous companionship. You arrived unexpectedly and when I needed you the most. Thank you to my family, blood and otherwise, for being steadfast supporters of my writing fixation from childhood. It is a thing of liberation to be heard unconditionally. The universe has bestowed upon me insurmountable luck in the form of my sisters and parents. Thank you to the first readers of this manuscript, who lent me their time and their words during the book's most nascent vulnerability. I appreciate you: Carolina Meurkens, Mayah Lovell, Maggie Von Sacher, Lucas Restivo, and Mack Gregg. Thank you to Morgan Bayona and Pearl Ernat for donating your time to making my cover visions come to life and to my dear little sister and fellow artist Maeve Scully for the portrait at the conclusion of this book. Thank you to Rita Rushanan and Sophia Gluskin-Braun for keeping me fed, housed, and loved while I ran off to write a memoir. Thank you to Lauren Woyczynski for sharing in my grief and in my love. Thank you to my editorial team at Stone of Madness Press for your steadfastness, patience, and felicitations. Thank you endlessly to the team at Gnashing Teeth Publishing for taking a chance on bringing this work to life. You have granted my greatest wish. And finally, thank you to everyone who is in this book and everyone who isn't.

About the Author

L Scully is a trans writer and double Capricorn currently based in the ether. L's chapbooks, *Like Us* and *100 I Love Yous*, are available from ELJ Editions and Ethel, respectively. They have been invited to artist residencies nationally and internationally and are a Best of the Net and Pushcart Prize nominee. Their work can be found widely in print and online in venues such as Jellyfish Review, Wales Art Review, and Boston Art Review. L recently completed their MFA in Creative Writing from Lesley University in Cambridge, MA. They are a winter swimmer and rescue dog parent.

Printed in the USA
CPSIA information can be obtained
at www.ICGtesting.com
JSHW061317281023
50805JS00009B/117